# VERMONT WILD

*Adventures of Fish & Game Wardens*

VOLUME 4

# VERMONT WILD

## Adventures of Fish & Game Wardens

VOLUME 4

Written by **Megan Price**

Cover by **Carrie Cook**

Illustrated by **Jacob Grant & Bob Lutz**

**Pine Marten Press**

# Pine Marten Press

### First edition

Copyright © 2016 by Megan Price

Designed by Carrie Cook

Printed by L. Brown and Sons
Barre, Vermont

For information and book orders, visit our website:
**www.PineMartenPress.com**

**ISBN: 978-0-98288729-5**

**Library of Congress Control Number: 2010934765**

## *Answers to your most pressing questions:*

### *Did the stories in this book really happen?*
A bull moose charge on a moonless night?
A warden fights five guys for their guns?
A terrified taxidermist turns federal witness?
An angry wife settles a hunting camp dispute?
A language barrier ends in longjohns?

*Trust me, I ain't clever enough to make this stuff up!*

### *Have some stories been embroidered just a little?*
A whole lot less than, "The one that got away!"

### *What about the characters?*
The wardens and deputy wardens are real.
Innocent bystanders names are used if they have
a sense of humor and swear they won't sue us.

### *What about the poachers?*
We change their names and some of the particulars
so's not to further embarrass their families.
Their shenanigans and convictions are real!

*Get ready, here it comes....*

## **Big Legalese Disclaimer**
Any resemblance to any individual,
living or dead, is one heck of a coincidence.

### *That's our story and we're sticking to it.*

# Dedication

*To my good friend,*
*W. Douglas Darby*

and

*To all who work to protect*
*wildlife and wild places*

*Thank you.*

For more "Wild" books visit:
www.PineMartenPress.com

# STORIES

"Let go! Give it to me," I heard Ken say.
"No!" the fellow in the passenger seat
growled back. I looked for a glint
of steel, for a gun.

# CADILLAC JACK

CONTRIBUTED BY JOHN KAPUSTA

 warden runs into all kinds of characters, and a foursome from down country ranks near the top of my strangest encounters.

I was with Deputy Warden Ken King near Cook Hill Road in Greensboro, waiting for night hunters. It was a little more than a week before the opening day of rifle season, but some guys like to cheat and get a jump on the season.

There was a well kept hayfield with some old apple trees along the tree line—a combination deer find hard to resist. I knew it was a popular spot with poachers and thought it might prove to be again this night.

I backed the truck into the brush well off the dirt road. Ken and I got out and draped a camo tarp over it to help hide the chrome bumpers, rear view mirrors and windshield from any spotter's light that might wash over us.

I was watching clouds slide by the stars and making another "to do" list in my head when I heard the unmistakable sound of tires rolling slowly over a dirt road off in the distance.

A car came down the road at a crawl, headlights off—and a light shined out the passenger's window onto the meadow about 300 feet away from us.

The beam swept the field slowly. I saw whoever was holding it had a steady hand.

"Looks like we got one," I said to Ken in a hushed voice. "We'll just watch a minute."

"Okay," he replied. We both looked hard to see if there was the muzzle of a rifle pointing out a car window. But they were just too far away to see that kind of detail.

My eyes followed their light beam. No eyes reflected back from the meadow. The light went dark. The vehicle kept coming at us.

About 100 feet from where we were hidden, the spotlight came on again. The beam swept across our truck. Even though I was sitting with my back partially hidden by a tree trunk, I instinctively turned my body into the shadows and held my breath.

You never know if light reflected off your badge or name tag might be just enough to give your presence away.

We were lucky. The light passed over and the car kept traveling at a snail's pace. When I was confident they were safely past us and didn't suspect a thing, I whispered to Ken, "Let's go get 'em!"

We got to our feet quietly, stayed low and rushed to pull the camo off the truck. Then we jumped in and launched into a classic game warden night chase—a crawl.

So far, all we had these guys for was a few seconds of shining a light. That's a violation, but I wanted to see what else they had in mind. Would they point a rifle out of the window? Shoot?

The more evidence they gave us, the better our case.

I didn't rush to catch up to these fellows. Ken and I were watching and taking mental notes. We studied shadows and did our best to learn how many people were in the car. We were looking for a rifle—maybe more than one— reaching out a window. Knowing these things could save your life.

My truck was made for night stalking. There were toggle switches to control all the lights. When I hunted poachers, it was total blackout. Headlights, parking lights, brake lights, dome light, dash lights—all lights were off.

I was counting on the people in that car to not look behind them, to get all caught up in looking ahead for deer.

Ken and I pulled closer to the suspect's rear bumper and when we did, I saw a Cadillac emblem on the center of the trunk—definitely not your typical deer jacking vehicle. And the license plate read Massachusetts, not Vermont.

Even under a dark night sky, this sleek car was impressive. The notion a poacher would use a Cadillac to jack deer threw me for a split second. Was the driver lost? Or was he just getting an early start on a funeral procession somewhere up the road?

I'd occasionally come across visitors with poaching on their "to do" vacation list. But never one driving what looked to be the latest model of America's most expensive passenger car.

Who would want to make a mess of a sleek black Caddy's trunk by putting a bloody deer carcass in it?

It made no sense. But all their actions said they were night hunting.

"How many do you see?" I whispered to Ken, referring to the number of car occupants. He had the clearest view of the passenger side. We needed to know all we could before making our move.

"Four total," Ken whispered back.

From the corner of my right eye, I saw Ken write down the car's license plate number. He knew the job well. If these guys discovered us tailing them and made a run for it, we might need it to track them.

I increased our speed a hair and got my truck just 10 feet from the Cadillac's rear bumper.

Then we waited for their searchlight to shine across another field.

"Meadow ahead," Ken whispered and I nodded.

"Get ready. You take the spotlight from the passenger. I'll get the driver," I whispered to Ken.

"Got it," Ken said quietly. He was like a bird dog ready to flush a grouse.

I pulled closer. My truck grill was just 18 inches from the Caddy's trunk.

Ken opened his passenger door slightly, looked at me, then back at the Caddy.

We rounded a wide curve that opened up on another field. Before us, the front seat passenger turned his searchlight on again, almost on cue.

"Go," I said quietly and Ken threw his door wide and bolted for the Caddy.

I toggled on my blue lights, headlights and the siren almost simultaneously to create a distraction. I wanted the Caddy crew to look back at me and not see Ken coming at them.

I punched the truck's brakes and threw it into park just a foot behind their taillights.

Their senses jolted by the noise and whirling lights, the Caddy passengers weren't prepared for Ken's big hands reaching inside their car like some zombie in a horror movie.

And now, it was my turn. I leaped out from behind the steering wheel and ran to the Cadillac driver's door.

I grabbed the door handle with my left hand and yanked it open, threw my right shoulder across the driver's chest and snagged the keys out of the car's ignition with my hand.

Generally, that would do it. With their vehicle disabled and wardens standing on both sides, weapons at the ready if needed, the fellows inside would just give up.

But not this time.

I heard the sounds of a struggle and saw hands and arms flailing in the passenger seat. An elbow came at my head and just missed punching me in the right eye.

The Cadillac's dome light was on but all I could see was the front seat passenger twisting back and forth. There was angry muttering. I recognized Ken's voice.

"Give it to me," Ken demanded.

Was Ken struggling to get control of a handgun?

"Game wardens! Halt!" I shouted, hoping to stop the tug of war before it escalated further.

My words didn't have much effect.

I heard Ken's boots scuffling on the gravel road and what sounded like a dog growling.

A dog?

Usually the guy holding the spotting light was so startled to see hands coming through the window, he would throw himself back into the seat and drop everything. He'd figure it was the Grim Reaper coming for him.

But not this time. What was going on with Ken?

The passenger seesawed back and forth in his seat. I pulled my head out of the Cadillac—the car turned off and the keys clutched tight in my right hand—stood up and looked over the car roof for Ken.

The spotlight was shining up at the stars, then down at the dirt. It created a big mix of bright light and deep shadows, making it tough to see clearly. But there was something else Ken and the man appeared to be fighting over.

I spotted pink skin, tiny feet with claws, white cotton balls the size of melons. It was being thrust in and out of the car window as Ken tugged on the spotlight and the passenger yanked back.

"Let go! Give it to me," I heard Ken say.

"No!" the fellow in the passenger seat growled back.

I looked for a glint of steel, for a gun or knife.

But that wasn't it. It was something else and it appeared to be caught up in the light's cord. It wriggled and twisted like a snake in the road.

I heard growling, jaws snapping and then a yip like someone mistakenly stepped on a puppy's tail.

Ken let out an "Ow!" but he kept hold of the light.

"Stop! Game wardens!" I shouted again.

The hands quit yanking the puff ball in and out of the car window just long enough for me to see a flash of white canine teeth and black button eyes. They were ringed wide with the white of doggie fright. And then I got it.

The passenger was trying to keep his tiny pooch from sailing out the window with the spotlight. He didn't want to lose his dog.

I bent down and shined my flashlight square in the guy's face and said, "Freeze!"

The passenger finally did what he was told. And the whole shootin' match went flying out the window into Ken's waiting arms—the light, a big long cord and a writhing, snapping poodle.

The driver and passengers threw up their hands and said, "Okay! All right! Don't shoot!" with thick Boston accents.

With the tug of war over, I looked closer at the four men. Once again, this crew had me silently shaking me head.

They were dressed in spotless suits, crisp white shirts and ties. Their haircuts were worthy of aspiring politicians.

And when I checked the backseat and floor for weapons, I saw they were all wearing shiny wingtips.

These fellows sure didn't fit my customary deer poacher portrait. But their actions did.

I told them to keep their hands up where we could see them. Then I asked Ken how he was doing.

"He bit me!" he said and shook his right hand like it was smarting.

The driver had a valid driver's license. All the fellows stepped out of the car one at a time so we could check them. Not one of them was carrying a firearm or a knife.

The little dog was separated from the long cord by the front seat passenger and Ken took the spotlight as evidence. When the big man got his dog back, he smiled and tucked it beneath his coat to calm it.

I popped the trunk and found two new rifles inside. Neither was loaded.

I asked the driver what they were doing in the area and he said they were just visiting. They gave the name of a local businessman who I heard wintered in Florida. The fellow said they were renting his place for a vacation.

I knew I'd have a hard time making a case to a judge. Writing this up would give the State's Attorney a good laugh, but I couldn't imagine him charging these guys with a crime. Still, I didn't want to tell these guys that.

So, I put the men on notice.

"I don't know what you fellows are up to, but it's against the law to shine a light at night to spot deer. I could arrest all of you, have your car towed and you four could spend the night in jail," I told them.

The driver immediately protested and the others chimed in too. "Geez, we're sorry. We didn't mean anything by it. We didn't know..."

I let them go on a minute or so and then said, "I don't want to see you doing this ever again. Got it?" I said looking each of them in the eye.

All four of them nodded like choirboys and said, "Okay. Thank you. Will do."

Even the little poodle wagged its tail in the arms of its owner, as it looked at me.

"All right then," I said sternly. "Turn on your headlights and drive carefully. If you want to hunt, buy a license, please."

The Cadillac pulled away slowly and Ken and I walked back to the truck. At last, I could focus on my deputy.

"Ken, are you okay?" I asked him as we climbed inside. "Let me see." I flicked on the interior lights and he held up both hands so we could look at the bite wounds. There were a couple of puncture marks and some swelling.

"Yeah, he just surprised me more than anything," Ken chuckled. "I sure didn't expect to get bit! I'll soak my hand in Epsom salts when I get home tonight. I should be fine."

"Well," I said to Ken, "That was a strange stop even without the poodle!"

From their choice of car, to their clothes, to the unloaded rifles in the trunk, to bringing a toy poodle along—the Cadillac crew left me believing their shining a light was just a prank.

I figured I'd never run into those guys again.

Boy, was I wrong.

*He bent low and wrestled the .22 out of
my hands while a taller fellow threw a
big roundhouse punch at my head.*

# BRUISIN' & CHEWIN'

CONTRIBUTED BY JOHN KAPUSTA

O pening day of rifle season dawned cold and wet with a driving north wind and the sting of sleet on my face.

I knew some hunters would hear the wintry mix slapping their camp windows and just pull their blankets tighter, roll over and stay in bed. They'd wait for the skies to clear before getting out into the woods.

But not game wardens. Deer season is the busiest time of the year for us. Hail, sleet or three feet of snow, we're out there watching.

This morning, an hour before dawn, I parked my cruiser in some thick cedars off a narrow trail in Greensboro.

I was headed to a long ridge that held a mix of field and hardwoods. The acreage saw many deer hunters trudging through.

Standing on top, I could cover a lot of miles with my field glasses, watching for hunters and listening for gunshots below.

When I heard a shot, I walked towards the sound to locate the hunter and their animal. I wanted to make certain the deer taken was found, tagged and the law followed.

It was a long day with fewer hunters than usual because of the weather.

On stormy cold days like this, some deer will seek out their own place to bed down and just wait out the storm like we humans.

But big bucks are out searching for does regardless of the weather.

As the sun was about to set, I headed to a logging road I knew. It was easier walking in the lengthening shadows.

I rounded a curve in the trail and spied three fellows walking single file, rifles over their shoulders, coming at me.

There was a Jeep with Massachusetts license plates parked at an angle on the side of the trail between us. I knew that narrow drive led to a summer camp. It would have been boarded up months earlier.

I called out to the men, "Hold up a minute!" and walked quickly in their direction.

When I got within eight feet of the hunters, I opened up my jacket to show them my badge, identified myself as a game warden and asked to see their hunting licenses.

The guy in front said, "Oh, sure," and started patting his coat pockets, then his trousers. The two other guys were watching him and within five seconds they were doing the same thing.

I stood there watching the three of them slap themselves as if they were battling ants from their shoelaces to their necks.

After 30 seconds of opening and closing numerous pockets, the first fellow said, "Oh geez, I must have left it back at the house."

"Yeah, me too," the second fellow said while the third mumbled something and then looked down at his boots.

"Well, why would you do that?" I asked the trio. "You're supposed to carry your hunting license with you. If you got a deer you'd want to tag it, right?"

The first fellow was clearly the leader. The other two guys opened their eyes wide, swallowed hard and looked at him for direction on what to do and say next.

Their leader didn't stumble.

"We were out in the woods this morning and got so wet, we went back to the house to change," he said. "I hung my clothes up to dry. I musta left my license inside my pants by mistake."

His buddies looked at me and nodded in agreement in a kind of silent, "What he said," confirmation.

Well, the explanation did make sense. It had been a cold, wet day. I was sure lots of guys had gotten soaked, found shelter and changed clothes before going back in the woods. But it didn't sound right to me that all three of them would make the same mistake.

You'd grab your wallet no matter where you were going and if you had a hunting license, it would be in there. Or it would be inside your hunting jacket.

One guy forgetting?  Maybe.  All three of them?
Not likely.

I was hungry, cold and bone tired, but the job
demanded I follow up.  The law said you have to
carry a valid hunting license on your person if
you are hunting.

And with the three of them out in the woods on
opening day of rifle season, each holding a rifle,
there wasn't much debate as to what they were
doing.

"Where are you gentlemen staying?" I asked
them.  They gave me the same address as the
city slickers with the cotton ball poodle that
had bitten Ken less than two weeks earlier.

"Hunh.  Small world," I thought.  But I didn't
say a word.

I looked more closely at their faces.  Were these
fellows related to the Cadillac crew?  The Boston
accent was the same, and the house they were
renting was the same, but I couldn't be certain.
It could be a coincidence.

"Tell you what I'm going to do, fellows," I said.
"You climb in your car and get warmed up.
I'm going to get my cruiser.  I'll meet you at the

bottom of the hill. Wait there for me. Then I'll follow you to your place and you can show me your hunting licenses."

The talker nodded in the affirmative and said, "Okay." The other two said nothing.

"All right," I said. "I'll meet you in 20 to 30 minutes. Wait for me."

I took off at a brisk clip towards my cruiser, glancing once or twice over my shoulder. I saw the trio lower their rifles and empty them.

It took me a good 15 minutes to get to my car, then another 10 minutes to drive around the mountain.

But when I pulled into the end of the trail there was nothing. I saw where lugged Jeep tracks had left fresh mud on the paved road. It was clear they had just driven away.

That didn't make me very happy. I'd told them to wait.

So I headed on over to where they told me they were staying—the home of a local businessman.

His was one of the nicest houses around, with stone pillars on either side of the paved driveway, each capped with a brass coach light. He had a paved driveway leading to the top of a hill with a panoramic view of the valley.

I wasn't so sure about these guys. I wondered to myself if the owner knew these fellows very well. The homeowner was a straight shooter.

I drove through the gates and up to the mansion and found the Jeep just outside the back door. They hadn't tried to hide their car.

I walked up the steps to the back door and knocked. I could see a couple men walking around inside. Each had a cocktail in his hand.

There was loud music and a television blaring in the background.

It sounded and looked like there was a party going on inside.

I knocked again, harder, and waited. Still nothing.

I tried one more time, with my fist balled up, smacking the door hard enough to rattle the knob.

No answer.

I knew they had to have heard the banging.
I guess they figured I'd just go away eventually.

They must be thinking of somebody else.

I decided I'd just invite myself in. One twist of
the knob was all it took. They hadn't bothered
to lock the door.

"It's Warden Kapusta. I'm here to check your
licenses," I shouted as I entered the home
through a mudroom into the showcase kitchen.

The long counter was littered with liquor and beer
bottles and a dozen open bags of chips and dip.

As I strolled past a man, his reaction was a
combination of "Do I know this guy?" and "Well,
hello! Pull up a chair. Make yourself a drink."

The radio was blaring. There was no point
in trying to talk. I followed the sound to the
source, found it beneath a counter and punched
a few buttons. It went silent.

The men who had been laughing and smiling
and shouting to one another above the din
turned and scowled at me.

"Hey! Whaz wrong wid you?" one of them growled.

I ignored him and walked quickly into the living room.

Now, it was just the TV I needed to silence so I could talk to this crowd.

I found a big screen broadcasting a football game and two more men. They were at opposite ends of a sectional leather couch and shouting at the players and coaches.

I walked over and stood in front of the television, blocking the action. These fans didn't like that.

"Hey! Whatcha doin'?" yelped the animated fellow standing at the back of the sofa.

An older fellow with a paunch reached for the remote. I saved him the trouble. I slid a hand behind me and turned the TV off.

The screen went black and the room went silent. Now, I had their full attention.

"I'm Vermont Fish and Game Warden John Kapusta. I'm here to check the hunting licenses of the three men I met hunting earlier," I said.

A fellow with a highball in his hand had sauntered into the living room to see why their world had gone quiet. There were four men before me now.

The hunters must have rushed home and jumped in the shower and changed. Gone was the hunting gear. All of them were dressed in casual clothes now.

I recognized two of the men before me, but one seemed to be missing.

I stood glaring at the group, waiting for them to act.

"Oh! Oh yeah!" one guy said, nodding to a buddy next to him. "The licenses!"

The two began wandering around the room like they were blindfolded and playing a game of Pin the Tail on the Donkey, arms grasping air.

They bumped into one another, and then went off in separate directions, pulling open a table drawer, flipping over seat cushions.

I saw something out of the corner of my eye. It was a younger man headed up the hallway towards me and the living room.

I recognized him as the third hunter.

He saw his friends wandering about digging into cabinets and looked over at me, puzzled.

"I'm here to see your hunting license," I said to him.

"Oh yeah," he replied like a bored teenager. He turned to his right, saw a display cabinet full of trophies and opened the door. He lifted the shiny awards up, one at a time, as if he expected his license to magically appear beneath one of them.

As the trio busied themselves like squirrels searching for nuts, I began looking about the room for the rifles they had been carrying.

I spied a glass fronted gun case in a corner of the living room and peered at the contents but didn't move my feet. I waited.

After a few minutes of poking about in the living room and kitchen, the men tired of humoring me by pretending to search for their hunting licenses. They drifted off. And one by one, I found them chatting and laughing with their buddies, sipping their cocktails and just ignoring me.

I decided I'd waited long enough for proof they had valid hunting licenses.

I walked over to the gun cabinet, opened the door and removed the rifles I had seen the trio carrying—two Marlin lever actions and a .22.

I turned and started to my cruiser with their guns.

Two of the guys saw me and sounded the alarm. I heard a beer can slam on a tabletop and a man yelled, "Hey! He's got our guns!"

I turned around and saw a big guy with knitted eyebrows blocking my path.

"Whadduh yous think yous doin'?" he snarled at me, his chest blown up and his hands balled into fists.

Hearing his voice and looking straight into the man's eyes, I was almost certain he was one of the fellows in the Cadillac, Ken and I had stopped earlier.

Another guy jumped to his feet and challenged me.

I stood firm, the three rifles in my arms. Then I spoke loud enough for the whole house to hear me.

"At least three of you fellows have been hunting deer without a license today. I'm taking the rifles you were carrying with me as evidence," I said. "I'm going to cite you."

I brushed past the two men and started towards the mudroom door.

Someone behind me muttered angrily, "I don't think so." I smelled booze and felt hot, moist breath on the back of my neck.

A hand slid under my elbow and grabbed at a rifle. I spun around and saw it was the young, wiry guy. He bent low and wrestled the .22 out of my hands while a taller fellow threw a big roundhouse punch at my head.

I ducked and the fist missed me, put the two rifles down, then stepped back to the living room wall and put up my fists. I didn't want anyone coming up from behind me again.

I clocked one guy under the chin.

He yelped and fell backwards knocking his buddy to the floor. I turned to the other two and their eyes went wide with fear.

I lunged forward and pushed them out of my way and took off down the hall after the thin guy with the .22.

He ducked into a room and slammed the door.

I tried the doorknob.  It was locked.  I banged the door open with my shoulder and saw the fellow sliding the .22 into the corner of a clothes closet.

I ran up tight behind him, reached around his back for the rifle and growled, "Give me the gun."

He muttered something under his breath, pushed the rifle deeper into the closet and tried to slam the door, to keep me out.

I stretched above his head, put my left hand up high to keep the door from closing and reached in with my other hand to snag the rifle.

He used the opportunity to elbow me hard in the ribs.  Then he spun around and began pounding my breadbasket like he was a prizefighter who just learned his girlfriend had cheated on him. He used my gut like it was his heavy bag.

I dropped my hands and went at him.

We wrestled, punched, jabbed and bounced off the bed.  We slammed and slid off all four walls for a good five minutes.  The closet door came off

its hinges and the rifle toppled and fell into the
room.

A standing lamp crashed to the floor and the
globe smashed into tiny pieces. A nightstand
collapsed when he landed on it. We each
threw some hard punches that missed and
the sheetrock paid for it with holes.

But it doesn't take long to tire when you're
battling that hard. In a desperate last ditch
effort to keep the .22, the skinny fellow cradled
the rifle in his elbows and began shimmying
beneath the double bed.

It was as if he was a World War I soldier trying
to crawl under barbed wire, back to the safety
of his foxhole. I couldn't believe my eyes.

I took a deep breath, bent down, grabbed him
by the ankles and dragged him back out.

He flipped over to take another swing at me
and when he did, I grabbed the .22 rifle away
from him.

I cocked my arm to give him another wallop.
He covered his face, went limp and shook his
head from side to side slowly, and whimpered,
"No more. No more."

"All right then. Keep it that way," I said to him.

I looked around for my hat, found it a little beat up but still good and put it on. Then I turned back to the man lying on the floor and said, "Get up, you're coming with me."

I had the young fellow walk ahead of me while I carried the .22 back down the hall and into the living room.

I felt a twinge of guilt as I exited that bedroom. I hoped the owner had gotten a big security deposit from these guys. It was a mess.

As I approached the living room, the sound of the televesion could be heard again—not anywhere near as loud as when I showed up—but it was clear this group could not tear themselves away from a game, no matter what.

When the football fans saw me walking down the hall behind their man, their mouths fell open. I got a distinct feeling they figured their guy would be victorious.

I walked to the spot I had left the other two rifles. I wasn't going to leave without them. But they were gone. I didn't make a fuss about it.

I decided to take the .22 to my cruiser and then return to have a chat with the fellows. They didn't try to stop me from leaving.

When I returned, I found all five men in the living room. The older fellow even hit the mute button on the TV. Finally, they appeared ready to listen to me.

I took a deep breath and said, "I tried working with you fellows earlier and you didn't listen. I could arrest all of you right now, for interfering with a law enforcement officer."

They looked at one another. The young guy who had battled me for the .22 was collapsed in an overstuffed chair. His left eyelid was swelling. His nose was dripping a thin trail of blood and he rubbed his jaw with his right hand as I spoke.

"I am going to cite the three men I saw hunting this afternoon for failing to provide a valid hunting license on demand of a game warden," I said. "And you are going to give me the other two rifles. Now."

I looked hard into the eyes of each of the men. The oldest fellow scowled, shook his head, looked over to the guy next to him and said, "Give him the guns."

That man jumped up, took four steps and reached behind a cabinet. He pulled out the two Marlins and brought them to me, then went and sat back down. He didn't say a word.

"Okay. Now, I want the three of you who I met in the woods to come on out to my cruiser and bring your IDs with you. I'm going to do the paperwork there. And let me be very clear. If any of you have any ideas about putting up more of a fuss, then all five of you are going to jail tonight. You got it?"

Four of them glanced over at the older man again. He was clearly the boss. He pursed his lips, looked them in the eyes and snarled, "Do what he wants. Now!" and turned back to watch the game.

Two of the fellows jumped to their feet and ran to get their coats. The brawler did the same, but at a slightly slower pace.

I waited while the men put their boots and coats on, the two other rifles in my arms. When the trio was assembled, I said, "After you," and off we went into the cold night air.

I placed the two rifles in the trunk and then told the men to get inside my cruiser. Citation book open and pen in hand, one by one I asked for

their identification and started filling out
the forms.

All three produced driver's licenses that
said their hometown was Old Oaken Bucket,
Massachusetts.  They each handed me birth
certificates and Social Security cards—all of it
brand spanking new.

I'm no geography expert, but I had never heard
of that Massachusetts town.

And, even stranger, the identification for all three
of these men looked like it had just come off a
copier.  You carry ID in your wallet, the edges get
bent, scuffed and worn.  But the paperwork these
fellows handed me was pristine—all of it.

Who carries their birth certificate with them to
just go from Massachusetts to Vermont?

I felt like something very strange was going on.
Like maybe they weren't who their documents
said they were.  But I didn't have the fancy
equipment available today to determine if they
were telling me the truth or not.

So, Old Oaken Bucket, or Bottom of the Well, I
had to cite them based on the identification they
gave me.

After I filled out their citations, I explained to them they would have to appear in court and if convicted of hunting without a license, pay a fine.

When they had paid their fine, they could ask for their rifles back. They didn't like this at all.

"We're just visiting for a few days. Isn't there some way we can get this over with now?" one fellow asked.

"Yeah! We don't want to have to come back. How about we pay a fine now? Isn't that good enough?" a second guy asked.

Well, in fact they could. Vermont had a system in place which allowed those charged with minor crimes like this to plead no contest or guilty, pay a fine in cash set by a judge, and mail it off to the court.

Do that and it was case closed. No need for a court appearance.

I explained the process required me to cite them in writing, call a judge to set the fine, have the men sign their citations with their guilty or no contest plea noted, add the cash and drop the whole thing in the mail.

"Yeah, yeah, yeah. That sounds good. We'll do that," the most talkative guy said with the other two nodding in agreement.

"Okay, let me see if I can get ahold of a judge. Just sit tight," I told them.

I got on my cruiser radio. A half hour later, a judge had set their fine at $150 each for hunting without a license, first offense. Now, it was time for them to pay up. "I need cash from each of you," I explained. "No checks."

The three of them flipped open their billfolds and peeled off a few bills from a stack that must have amounted to a few thousand dollars in each wallet.

Two of the fellows had trouble finding bills as small as a $50. They said they needed to go back in the house to have a friend make change.

I was thinking maybe I ought to call Dispatch to see if anyone had robbed a bank in New England recently.

These guys were high rollers. Why in the world were they up in the woods of Greensboro hunting, but too cheap to buy hunting licenses?

I didn't want to have to chase all three of
them again.

"One of you fellows can go in to get change.
The other two, you stay right here," I said.  "And
make it quick."  If they all went inside I might
have to battle to get the trio back in my car.

"Okay," the talker said.  "I'll go.  I'll be right
back."  He kept his word.  He was back in less
than five minutes.

With all three of them in my cruiser—two in
the backseat and one sitting beside me, I said,
"Okay, I'm driving you all to the closest post
office.  You're going to drop that envelope in the
mail.  Then I'll bring you back here."

The three of them nodded like choirboys.
I turned the cruiser around and headed to
the Greensboro Bend Post Office.

As I was about to turn onto the main road, I
caught a flash of silver in my rear view mirror.
The fellow who ran inside had taken a couple
sticks of gum, stuck them in his mouth and
started chewing.

He elbowed his buddy and that fellow took some
sticks, unwrapped them and started chewing too.

We rode in silence except for the smack, pop,
slurp and chomp of the men in the backseat.
It was irritating, but I figured maybe they were
trying to quit smoking or nervous.

I parked the cruiser and before the crew got out,
I turned on the dome light and counted the cash
one more time—all $450 of it.

Then I licked the envelope's glue seal and
pressed down real hard and held it a few
seconds. I made certain it was sealed shut
before I handed it to them.

"All right, go on and drop it in the box," I told
them. "I'll wait."

I sat in the cruiser, headlights on, watching
them. The trio walked to the mailbox so slowly
you would have thought there was a firing
squad waiting for them.

Their backs were towards me, but I could
see heads turn. They were chatting about
something. I looked down at my watch. It was
close to 9 p.m.

By the time I got home, it would be too late to
return many of the calls I knew awaited me.
I wanted a hot shower, supper and some sleep.

I needed to be back out in the woods early
again tomorrow.

I wished these guys would hurry up. They finally
made it to the mailbox but appeared to be just
standing there. I was running out of patience.

"Just drop it in there and get on back here,"
I mumbled to the empty seats. "Let's go!"

Have they changed their minds? Still they
stood there talking.

Exasperated, I stepped out of the cruiser and
began walking towards them. One of the guys
spotted me and elbowed his buddy hard. All
three heads shot up like wild turkey poults
who sensed a prowling fox.

Now, the trio couldn't get back to me fast
enough. They left the mailbox in a hurry,
elbows pumping. One guy had a funny look
on his face, like a kid exiting the kitchen with
a mouth stuffed full of cookies.

"What are these guys up to now?" I asked
myself. "Is there another card up their sleeve?"

"You fellows stop right there," I told them as
they approached me. I pointed to the sidewalk,

"Just stay put and don't move."

I walked over to the mailbox and confirmed the lid was shut tight. They hadn't propped it open. It appeared fine.

I glanced back at them and saw the trio was standing almost shoulder to shoulder—watching my every move. Not talking. Their body language told me they were up to something. But what?

I peered closer at the drawer handle under the streetlamp. Nothing was amiss.

I looked back over at them again. They were still staring at me in silence. It was like they were waiting for me to spot something.

So, I took a third look, trying to figure out what they could have done.

It was a cast iron mailbox. The lid was shut tight. I knew they didn't have time to saw a hole in it or bury the envelope somewhere.

I bent closer, my nose just six inches from the lid. I turned my head to try and catch the streetlight better, to erase the shadows.

My flashlight was back in the cruiser.

Finally, I noticed something odd—a tiny bit of white—no bigger than the nail on your pinky finger. It was poking out like a tiny nose from under the lid's heavy cast iron corner, on the lower right side.

"What is that? Is that a piece of envelope? Maybe an envelope with cash in it?" I thought.

I stepped back, stood up, took a deep breath and reached for the tiny triangle as if I was a surgeon reaching inside a man for a piece of shrapnel next to an artery.

Ever so lightly, I pinched the tiny tail with my right thumb and index finger. Once I grasped it, I held it like a vise.

Then I reached over with my left hand and took hold of the drawer handle and slowly pulled the lid towards my chest—an inch, then two, then three.

I peered inside the lid and found myself looking at a fat, familiar envelope.

I gave the white corner a teensy tug, like a night fisherman feeling a baited line for a catfish.

The envelope didn't budge.

That was weird. It should be fighting me to fall down into the slot and disappear. How was the heavy packet just hanging there?

I took another deep breath and pulled straight up. And that's when I saw how they pulled yet another stunt—or attempted to anyhow.

There was a stretchy pink glob connecting the envelope to the mailbox lid. And now I got it. All that gum chomping on the way down here in the back of my cruiser wasn't nerves, but it was definitely nervy.

These guys intended to rush on back here after I dropped them off, grab their cash and tear up the citations. For all I knew, their pals might be hiding around the corner in the Jeep waiting for me to leave so they could recover the cash.

Well, I had to admit it was a clever move. Just not clever enough.

I gazed at the trio standing 30 feet away in the orange glow of the streetlight. They had their hands in their pockets, collars up against the cold, eyes locked on me.

I glared at them like a teacher who has seen it all before. The "I'm so disappointed in you boys" face, combined with "Did you really think you were going to put one over on me?"

I pulled a tissue from my front pants pocket and scraped the gum from the back of the envelope. I wadded up the tissue and stuffed it back in my pocket.

I raised the envelope up above my head and waggled it a couple times so all three could see it clearly. I pulled the mailbox slot wide open with my left hand and dropped the fat packet down into the mouth with my right. Their money was swallowed faster than a mackerel at Sea World.

Just for fun, I opened and closed the lid slowly several times, letting it slam shut. I wanted to be certain their cash and guilty pleas were irretrievable. And I wanted the trio to hear their fines being paid.

I walked back towards them and without stopping, nodded and said only, "Let's go home, Gentlemen."

They didn't make a peep all the way back to their rental. No gum chewing either. When we arrived, I got out and popped the trunk and handed them back their rifles. As far as I was concerned, it was case closed.

But I did leave them with one last piece of advice before they walked inside. "If you men want to hunt in Vermont, just buy yourselves hunting licenses before you step into the woods. I'll be watching you."

Two days later, I turned up their driveway before dawn. I wanted to know if they were still around. It had snowed a few inches the night before. The day promised to be cold and clear with no wind—perfect for deer hunting.

Their Jeep was gone. There were no lights on. The mudroom door was locked. It looked like they'd left town.

I climbed back into my cruiser and drove away thinking, "I guess these guys weren't serious about deer hunting after all. That or they've gone to get more gum."

The little boy's head shot up.
He had been listening intently, waiting
for his chance to say something.
When he heard me say "rifle" and "deer"
his eyes lit up.

# Button Up

Contributed by Eric Nuse

It was early July when I got a tip about fresh venison sizzling on the grill at a family's Lake Elmore weekend parties.

Since deer season was months away, the news raised my eyebrows.  It's not unusual for someone to take venison from their freezer, thaw, marinate and serve it up for family and friends.  Frozen and thawed means they would have downed the deer the previous year.

But if the venison served at this party was fresh, that meant someone was poaching.

I'd responded to calls of shots fired in the night along the nearby La Cass Road a week earlier, but found nothing.  With this new information, it seemed the two might be related.

I could be on to a poacher.

But was the poacher someone local who just dropped in and put some slabs of deer meat on the grill to share?  Or was it a summer camper renting a place at Lake Elmore?

I knew I had my work cut out for me. Campers are like nomads.  They tend to share cars, boats, food and drinks.  Some even move from one camp to another.  It's all part of the fun of living on a lake for the summer.  They can be a very close knit bunch.

If someone was brazen enough to place a platter of grilled fresh venison out for family and friends, he must be pretty confident no game warden would ever catch him.

This fellow might have a dozen refrigerators, coolers and freezers at the lake available to him.

He might even be borrowing a vehicle to do the poaching.

To add to my challenge, the clock was ticking. In August campers would be packing up and heading for their primary homes, getting the kids ready for school.  Adults would be settling back into their work schedule.

I visited the town clerk's office and looked at the Grand List, which provides the addresses and owners of all local real estate. One staff member guessed I was looking to buy a place there. I didn't tell her anything different.

I learned there was a big family that owned close to a dozen camps, rented some, and vacationed together at the lake each summer.

Grandparents, aunts, uncles, inlaws and cousins came from all over the country for a lengthy family reunion to renew old ties, I was told.

The original family name was Jackson, but with marriages and divorces factored in, I found myself jotting down more than a dozen surnames with Jackson family connections.

Of course, I didn't focus only on this family. But the fact the caller said the party brought together dozens of people, had me thinking maybe a member of the Jackson clan was connected.

It only makes sense that when you bring 50 to 100 people from several generations together, there's bound be a few characters among them.

I left the town offices with a long list. To narrow down my search, I compared the property owners to Department records of people previously convicted of fish and game violations, specifically deer poaching.

Bingo. Two men with the last name of Jackson had been prosecuted for taking deer out of season.

One owned a camp on the lake.

But I didn't get too excited. The convictions were nearly 15 years old. I realized those men could be grandparents by now.

It's a lot of work moving a dead deer, picking it up and loading it into a car trunk or having to lift it even higher onto a truck bed.

Hauling it out of a vehicle and cutting up the carcass will also have you working up a sweat. And none of this is work you want to take days to do when there's a good chance a game warden is tracking you, about to knock on your door.

So, deer poaching is usually a young man's game. And those were the campers I decided I should focus on.

I needed to do that without tipping anyone off as to what I was doing. In a small community, where most everyone is related to everyone else, that's not easy.

Five days later, I was rousted out of bed with another call about a shot in the night, this one over in Wolcott. I raced over there.

I found where a deer had been shot and dragged from a field. But there were no shell casings and no witnesses who could help me build a case.

I could only wonder if this deer jacking tied back to the Lake Elmore party platter.

I decided to stake out some Lake Elmore camps by sitting up on a hill adjoining the cemetery off Route 12. From there, you have a great view of much of the lake.

With field glasses and a more powerful scope to zoom in closer if I saw something interesting, I sat and watched campers come and go.

I was looking for any clue that might get me closer to convincing a judge to give me a search warrant.

How do wardens spot the man or family moving many pounds of illegal venison?

People who are guilty tend to look over their shoulders a lot and act nervous. And if you stuff a cooler full of deer meat, it is going to be very heavy. It might take a couple people to carry it up or down stairs.

And even though it sounds too good to be true, sometimes guys just drop the cooler and the contents go spilling out all over the road.

A man lugging a heavy cooler in or out of a camp at dawn or dusk when not many other people are outside, is one clue. Or maybe a fellow is acting nervous, looking all around, moving quickly while going to his car or camp. Maybe a guy puts a cooler in his car trunk or on a truck floor and then covers it up with tools or a tarp and drives away a little too fast.

Any of this behavior would be suspicious. It would make me think a fellow might have something to hide and I should watch him more closely.

I wrote down license plate numbers and descriptions of who got behind the wheel and with whom and in what vehicle. I spent hours trying to put things together.

I had asked the informant to call me with any additional information. Four days after my night run to Wolcott, he did.

He told me he'd attended another Elmore gathering as the guest of a Jackson distant cousin who was staying at the lake.

Once again, there was fresh venison steak being served. He said it was piled high for the adults right next to the potato salad and hotdogs.

The fellow holding a spatula at the grill even tried to convince the kids that venison burgers tasted better than beef, he said.

I asked for a description of the chef. My tipster said the grill master was average build, maybe 34 years old, clean cut with black hair and close to 6 feet tall. No tattoos.

He said he didn't talk to the guy, just listened. But he heard someone call the chef "Jerry."

His buddy told him Jerry grew up in Vermont, but had moved to Connecticut for work. He said Jerry was renting a camp somewhere across the lake against the ledges. He didn't know the number.

I thanked the caller, hung up the phone and smiled. I was getting closer. But I also knew I was running out of time. The calendar read August 3rd. The great summer camp exodus was starting. Families would be packing up and heading home to get their kids ready for school.

Jerry wasn't the only suspect, but he clearly was involved. I ran down my list of family members and smiled when my index finger landed on a camp owner named Jerome Jackson.

I checked his name with Department records and learned he had earned a hunting license as a teen, had reported six bucks over 18 years.

So, he was a former Vermonter and proven deer hunter who had moved down country to work.

But was he also a poacher?

I grabbed my Grand List notes. There he
was: Jerome and Monica Jackson, his wife, I
presumed, and the camp address.

I had a hunch this fellow was my poacher.
But if not, he knew who was.

It was time to take a closer look at Jerry's
summer home.

I drove along the lake in my family car,
wearing casual clothes to look his camp over
without being obvious. There were vehicles
stacked tight to both sides of the road
shoulders bearing license plates from New
Jersey, Maryland, Virginia, Connecticut and
Massachusetts.

The bottleneck gave me a great excuse to drive
slow and rubberneck.

I spotted Jerry's camp up against a steep
ledge, with long stairs leading to a screened
front porch. The sun glinted off it, making it
tough to see inside.

His was an older cottage with tiny windows.
Neighboring camps were so close, it was like a
peanut butter and jelly sandwich.

It would be just about impossible to walk between the cabins and not be seen or heard. I knew these camps would have back doors, probably with garbage pails that might hold some interest for me, but there was no way I could get to them.

Then I saw "No Trespassing" signs tacked beneath the cedars along the road. That clinched it. I was looking at Lake Elmore's Fort Knox.

It was time for Plan B—the "Yes, there's a game warden in the area, but he's not watching you" ploy.

For the next few days, I patrolled the lake by boat, checking fishing licenses and registrations and making certain everyone was carrying life vests.

And wherever I floated, I made certain I could see the comings and goings in Jerry's cabin and any guests who stopped by.

Jerry appeared to be married with two young children, a girl and a boy. There were trips made with their car for play dates and groceries, but I didn't see anything suspicious.

Dawn and dusk found me back in the
cemetery with my binoculars. I found a quiet
spot away from the gravestones to sit with my
back up against a tree.

I watched for anyone or anything out of the
ordinary.

I needed real evidence if I was going to be
able to get a search warrant and get into that
camp.

Days passed and despite hours of surveillance,
I had nothing but a deeper tan from my lake
patrols and a gut feeling Jerry was a poacher.

Lake Elmore's campers were like bees before
the first frost. Adults were pulling camp docks
out of the water, storing canoes and life vests
beneath their decks. A few were even hauling
their boats out of the water and winterizing the
engines.

I saw it all from the hilltop. What I didn't see
was the evidence I needed.

As the sun set over the ridge Friday evening,
I knew Saturday morning was likely my last
chance.

If Jerry or a neighbor had venison in their camp refrigerators, they would take it with them, maybe even give some away.

If I got really lucky, Jerry or Monica might be feeling generous tomorrow morning—handing out baggies of fresh venison to family and friends as a goodbye gift, in plain view, right by the side of the road.

I got up before dawn on Saturday, drove over to the cemetery, grabbed my binoculars and scope, hiked in and got comfortable.

I'd stood in the same spot so often, the grass was beaten down like a welcome mat.

There was thick fog on some of the lake surface below me.  It was a little after 6 a.m. I figured with Jerry and the wife having to pack and get the kids up, they wouldn't be out of their camp until 8 a.m. at the earliest.

I settled my back against the tree, raised my binoculars and peered at Jerry's camp.

My heart sank.  The station wagon I'd seen the couple drive was missing.  I grabbed my spotting scope for a closer look at the camp. Plywood was tacked up over the porch door.

My prime suspect had disappeared. Jerry and the family had left Lake Elmore. I'd missed my last chance to get evidence as they cleaned the place out and packed up their car.

Why did they leave so early? Had someone tipped him off I was watching? Connecticut was only a few hours away. They could've left in the early afternoon and still easily made it home before dark.

I sighed, kicked the grass beneath my boot and shook my head at my latest bout of bad luck. I took a full 30 seconds to sit there and feel sorry for myself.

Then I stood up, dusted off my trousers and told myself to get over it. There was plenty of other work to do. The family would be back here next summer. If I got more reports of poaching, I could try again.

I trotted down the slope, climbed into the cruiser and sat there a minute struggling to come up with anything else I could do now to solve this case.

And that's when I had a wild idea.  If this was football, I was about to make a Hail Mary pass.

The popular Wayside Restaurant was a half hour drive south, in Montpelier.  I would expect the couple to jump on the interstate there.

The Wayside was family friendly with good prices, fast service and a big parking lot. Having breakfast there would be a lot easier than cooking, washing dishes, then packing them.  Maybe the parents cajoled the kids into getting up in the dark with a promise of pancakes there?

If Jerry was at the diner, I could check his car for strands of deer hair and dried blood on the bumper.  It was public space.  No search warrant needed.

It was a total long shot.  But I had put so many hours into this case, I would have driven all the way to Connecticut and staked out the family's house if I thought my boss would let me.

I turned on my cruiser, pointed it towards the diner and hit the gas.  I took a few deep breaths and told myself I shouldn't let this case get to me, no matter how it turned out.

I'd driven maybe six miles, when I saw a car off to the side of the road and its signal lights flashing distress up ahead. I slowed down, looked harder and couldn't believe my eyes.

It was a station wagon with a license plate I had memorized.

Standing outside the wagon were my chief suspect and his wife. The kids—a girl aged six or seven and a boy maybe three or four years old—were off in the tall grass catching bugs.

I could not believe my good luck.

I toggled on my blue lights, and pulled over onto the road shoulder. I'd help them if I could, but I was also going to take a hard look at their car.

Jerry had popped the hood and when I stepped out of my car, I saw steam billowing up. It looked like an engine cooling problem of some kind. All that gear inside and on top of the wagon might have pushed a radiator hose or fan belt over the edge.

As I stepped out of my cruiser, I was enveloped by heat and noticed the humidity had risen too.

It was going to be a scorcher.

The couple turned to face me. Mom saw me
first and she elbowed her husband in the
ribs and pointed towards me like she was
looking at an approaching bandit.

Jerry's eyes got as big as saucers and his
hands started flapping against his front
pants pockets like a penguin. If a stranded
motorist has an officer of the law stop to
offer assistance, they're relieved, right?
They smile and welcome you. Not here.

Jerry composed himself and walked
towards me like he was the pastor of a
church welcoming a potential member.
I had the distinct feeling he was trying
to keep me away from his vehicle.

I sidestepped him and just kept sauntering
towards his car. His smile disappeared
and now he was on my heels, talking up a
storm.

"Uh, something gave way. The thermostat
or water pump seal, I guess," he said with
his voice a little shaky. "A tow truck is
coming."

I nodded, but I didn't say a word. I just let him keep talking.

The wife called out, "Careful," to the kids who were running in towards the car from the meadow. My arrival was more interesting than catching grasshoppers and picking wildflowers.

I glanced under the car hood, saw the coolant dripping and nodded as Jerry continued to talk about his radiator.

Then I stood up and walked down the side of the wagon, along the right of way, looking in the windows. I said, "You're hauling quite a load," and looked Jerry in the eye.

The young ones were now with their parents— the boy hanging onto his dad's pant leg and the girl trailing a finger through the dust on the front quarter panel. She was holding tight to her mom's skirt and pretending not to be interested in me.

The kids didn't speak, but appeared to have trouble keeping their feet still.

It was then I saw a rifle barrel poking out from beneath a quilt in the backseat.

It looked to be a .30 caliber with a light gathering scope—very handy for dusk or dawn hunting.

Why would you bring a deer rifle and scope to spend a few lazy summer weeks on Lake Elmore?

I saw beads of sweat forming on the driver's brow. He bit his lip. He was rocking side to side a bit—like a bigger version of his son. The boy was dragging a sneaker toe in the pea stone gravel and looking up intently at his dad and me.

Sometimes not saying anything gets people to tell you a lot. They want to fill the awkward silence. I had a feeling not talking much to this guy would work to my advantage.

Sure enough. I hadn't been quiet for more than a lightning strike count of 10 when he started telling me his life story.

"We're headed home to Connecticut. My people are from here and we come on up every summer to spend time with the family. The kids have lots of fun and get to know their cousins," he said before turning back to look at the engine.

"I guess I should have had it checked out by a mechanic before I left," he sighed. "It's been a good car, but the mileage is getting up there."

I nodded and walked to the back of the wagon, pausing to peer into the rear windows and study the contents.

I had never been this close to the family car before. At the lake, I couldn't take a chance on his relatives or friends seeing me and telling him about it.

Now, I was determined to give their vehicle a thorough visual inspection.

I glanced over at the couple and saw Jerry's head jerk up and a flash of concern come over the wife's face too. The little girl and her brother stuck close to their parents, watching me.

Each of the kids had button front sweaters on—the girl over a cotton print dress and the boy over his shirt and jeans. The two little ones were watching my every move, while crawling on their parents like a vine.

I tapped on the wagon's window, stood up, looked at Jerry and asked, "Is that a deer rifle?"

The little boy's head shot up. He had been listening intently, waiting for his chance to say something. When he heard me say "rifle" and "deer" his eyes lit up.

Finally, we had hit on a topic he knew something about.

He let go of his dad's leg, stood up tall and looking into my face said proudly, "Daddy got three deer this summer with that rifle."

He took a breath and added, "We're gonna have a big deer cook out for daddy's friends when we get home."

I saw the wife's free hand clench her skirt and twist it like she was wringing out laundry. Her knuckles went white and her lips pursed tight as a scar.

She looked down at her daughter and from the side of her mouth hissed, "Get your brother to button up!" and gave the girl a little push towards the boy who was looking up at me with a proud smile.

The girl looked confused, but took a faltering step towards her brother. She bent down and began buttoning up his sweater like he was one of her dolls.

I nodded, looked at both adults and asked, "Mind if I pop the hatch and look inside your vehicle?"

Jerry stood silent, thinking it over. Monica stared at him like he was a spider she was thinking of hitting with a flyswatter.

"I can get a search warrant if you want. It will just take longer," I told them.

Knowing the jig was up, Jerry's head fell to his chest and he sighed.

He pulled the car keys out of his pocket, hit the fob to unlock the hatch and said quietly, "Go ahead."

"Thank you," I said. I lifted the tailgate and pulled the quilt back slowly to take a closer look at the rifle.

There wasn't just one deer rifle hidden there, there were two—one with a light gathering scope and one without. And both were expensive foreign models.

I picked the rifles up one at a time and opened the chambers to make certain there were no shells inside. They were both empty. I dug deeper into the pile, but found only toys, clothes and beach bags.

I moved on to the backseat, where the boy and girl had been buckled into their car seats. Once again, blankets and quilts.

But on the floor, where the kids would dangle their feet above them, were coolers—big ones. I felt like a treasure hunter about to open the chest of riches he'd been promised.

Before I dug into the first cooler, I glanced back at the couple. I saw Monica elbow Jerry sharply in the ribs and mutter to him under her breath.

I couldn't hear her. But I had a pretty good idea it was along the lines of, "I told you not to kill those deer!"

I found bags of ice lying on top of more than 60 pounds of venison, all neatly sealed in freezer bags and labeled in black marker: roast, steaks, stew meat.

I walked to the other side of the car and opened that cooler. Same story. More ice, more venison.

I took a deep breath and began tugging on a cooler to remove it. Jerry said, "Wait a second. Let me help you." I thought that was nice of him.

I took their coolers and rifles to my cruiser. I had Jerry sit beside me in the front seat while I filled out the paperwork.

I explained I could take him to jail. But instead, I would give him a citation that would require him to return to Vermont and appear for his court date.

I knew his strong family ties to the area, along with not wanting to lose his expensive rifles, were a virtual guarantee he would return.

Jerry listened to me, then turned his head slightly, like he was considering his options. I followed his gaze out the windshield. He was looking at his wife. Monica's arms were crossed and she was glaring at him.

He looked like he might just prefer to go to jail rather than face her.

He paused, then said, "I guess the ticket is the best way to go. Yes. Thank you."

As I handed the citation to Jerry the yellow flashing lights of a tow truck appeared.

I decided I might be able to help the driver by directing traffic.

When I opened my cruiser door, I felt the late summer heat. It must have been 90 degrees. Cicadas were humming.

I was glad the family would be off the highway, out of the sun and on their way soon.

The little ones saw the tow truck and began jumping up and down, giggling with anticipation. Their mother reached for their hands and told them to stand with her.

Several cars came down the road, along with an older model pickup that looked like it was one winter away from the junkyard.

The drivers all hit their brakes and swung wide to accommodate the wrecker.

Jerry and I, Monica and the kids—we all
stood in silence as the big truck backed up
to the broken down wagon's bumper.

When the tow truck operator jumped out of
his cab, the little boy broke the silence.

He looked up into his mother's face, pinched
a button on the front of his sweater, tugged
at it and said, "Momma, it's hot. Can I
unbutton now?"

My job done, I tipped my hat and wished
the family a safe journey.

I held my hands out in front of the flame and ran them back and forth like a chef putting the crunchy crust on a tasty crème brûlée.

# You Broke It...

Contributed by Bob Lutz

There are women who think GPS—global positioning system—was created just so men would never have to ask for directions.

There's probably a kernel of truth in there. A lot of men don't like asking anyone for help.

And game wardens? We'd do just about anything to avoid admitting we needed a hand.

When I was in uniform, a big reason for this was the fact our message would be broadcast over public airwaves, through the Dispatcher who relayed calls.

"Warden Lutz requests assistance," would be heard by anyone with a police scanner. Thousands of civilians owned them and many people listened in—day and night.

So, get your car stuck somewhere in the woods chasing a guy and have to ask to be towed?

You could expect to be razzed by friends and complete strangers for months to come.

Getting yourself out of sticky situations was a point of pride. We were expected to be able to take care of ourselves and that meant our equipment too.

However, first and second generation snowmobiles made living up to this ideal especially challenging. They were heavy, tough to steer, underpowered and famously unreliable.

Wardens worked the machines hard, got stuck often, broke down often and walked out of the woods after dark, often.

But the machines improved. And in the early 1990s, I was one of the lucky guys upgraded to a 1980s era Artic Cat Jaguar. The machine was used, but I didn't care. It was a vast improvement over the 1970s sled I'd been riding.

The 340cc free air Jag had more power, improved steering, and a comfier seat. Oh sure, you still had to yank a cord to start it, but youth and an intact rotator cuff made that no problem at the time. I felt like I'd won the lottery. I looked at the winter ahead with a smile. I was convinced my job would be easier and a lot more fun.

Finally, I had a snow machine that would give me a fighting chance when a snowmobiler tried to outrun me.

Even better, the Cat was a lot lighter than my other sled.  I knew I could easily muscle the new snowmobile out of deep snow when I got it stuck. In a warden's life, stuck happens a lot.

Checking deeryards, visiting trap lines, searching for lost skiers and hikers?  Wardens have to make their own paths.

But, of course, the Jag designers had to make a few sacrifices to come up with a lighter, faster machine.

Something had to go.  And some engineer somewhere decided it would be the engine fan.

Briefly, that fan sucks in fresh air and blows it over a running engine, helping cool it.  All modern cars have engine fans and radiators too.  The combination prevents your motor from melting into a very expensive paperweight when you are stuck in traffic.

But whoever designed the Jag decided if it was cold enough for snow, it was cold enough to cool the engine.  And it kind of made sense.  At least on paper. And for most owners, it worked. But wardens are rough on their machines. We tend to push them to their limits.

I learned quickly my Jag ran best in temperatures where snot freezes and your eyeballs rattle in your skull like dried peas.

However, when the temperatures rise is when throngs of cabin fever refugees rush outside to ice fish, cross country ski, snowshoe and even sun themselves on the ice.

For me, those warm winter weekends meant hours of patrolling lakes and ponds on the Jag. I wanted to make certain people were safe.

But higher temperatures made the Jag a reluctant partner.

I learned fast to never let the engine idle. And when I thought I had pushed the machine too hard, I ran to the closest snow bank, threw open the hood and packed handfuls of snow on top of the engine.

It probably looked to some people like I was trying to build a redneck steam bath. But I was just trying to save myself from walking home and worse—making the dreaded call for help.

But one fine Spring day, while trying to move three deer carcasses from Lake Carmi to a disposal site I'd set up, I asked too much.

I parked at the fishing access and drove the Jag a mile up the lake. I noticed the surface was a little slushy. The ice beneath the track was melting. That meant the machine had to work harder. Still, I figured if I got the job done quickly enough, I'd be okay.

I briefly considered moving just one or two deer at a time, to lighten the load. But I had a long list of things to do this day and not a lot of gas in the tank. I didn't want to take the time.

So, I tied a rope from my bumper to each of the deer and cinched the three carcasses together one after the other—like a fish stringer. Then I jumped back aboard the snowmobile, headed for the quiet, swampy end of Lake Carmi.

I knew 300 plus pounds of dead deer, along with all my gear and me, was asking a bit of the sled. But I thought it could work.

I hadn't factored in the unusually balmy day.

I jumped aboard, gave the Jag some throttle and immediately noticed the machine was not happy hauling this much weight. I had to bear down on the gas just to get the Jag to move.

Out on the ice, I looked back over my shoulder and saw the dead deer were tossing water like fallen water skiers being dragged along.

Suddenly, towing three carcasses at once didn't seem like such a good idea.

But now, I didn't dare stop. All around me were pockets of water and some scary surface cracks. I started calculating the weight I was hauling. There was the machine, me, gear, three drenched dead deer and a swelling slush pile.

I realized I was sitting atop the weight of a small car. If I stopped on this rotting ice, I could easily punch a hole straight through and sink to the bottom.

I considered turning wide to head for the closest shore. But trying to turn with all that weight on the back might cause the sled to stall out.

I gritted my teeth, crouched low behind the windshield—and started muttering, "Please, get me to shore. Please, get me to shore..." like the sled was a friend I could rely on.

I felt the engine slowing. I pegged the throttle.
The engine screamed louder, but the track
acted like I was sledding through concrete.

A zip down the lake that would take me a
couple minutes on a frosty February day turned
into more than 10 minutes of lip biting lunacy.

When the Jag's skis finally crossed into the reeds
and swampy ground, I was one happy warden.

I let off the gas, turned the skis to head into
some alders. Then I punched the gas again to
head straight to the pit.

The smell of the hot engine filled my nose.
And did I detect plastic melting too?

Not to worry. Just 100 more feet, straight on,
and I'd be there. I'd unload these deer, roar
back down the lake and be done.

But the engine coughed. And then it quit.
I figured it had to be the heat. I jumped off,
threw up the hood and went to digging snow
and tossing it onto the cylinder heads like a
starved coyote diving for a field mouse.

I threw handfuls of snow on the engine. The
Jag threw them back like a girlfriend tossing your

love letters at you. The snow sizzled, turned into
spitballs of boiling water and leaped off in all
directions, like fleas on a wet dog.

"Hunh. Never seen the engine this hot," I
muttered.

I kept throwing snow and watching it vaporize
until I looked down and saw I was standing in
a couple inches of water.

This cool down was clearly going to take longer
than usual.

I shook my head, reached for my knife and
walked over to the Jag's rear bumper and cut
the deer carcasses loose.

The slush and strain on the rope had about
fused the knot in the line. I knew from
experience I'd be out here another 20 minutes
trying to untie the knots. A sharp knife is a lot
faster solution. Yeah, you end up with a shorter
rope, but I was in a hurry. Rope was cheap.

In retrospect, I shouldn't have been so
concerned with saving those minutes.

I dragged the deer, one at a time, into the
alders, putting six to 10 feet between each

carcass. That way the diners—crows, buzzards, fox, mice, coyotes, maybe even bear—would not have to fight as hard for a place at the table. There were many creatures that would benefit from the unfortunate deer, killed by dogs.

I walked back to the Jag and dropped more snow on the cylinders. Finally, there were no more spitballs thrown back at me.

I checked my watch and decided to give the motor five more minutes. I used the time to reach into my breast pocket to review the list of other projects I had planned to do this day.

The list was always more than I could get done in a week, but looking at it helped keep me focused.

Impatient after three minutes, I jumped up, lowered the hood, climbed aboard the Jag's footboards, turned the key on and yanked the recoil rope.

I got lots of "blug blug blug blug" but no "vroom."

I didn't see how I could have flooded the engine, but you never know.

I paused, pulled, pulled and pulled some more. I looked inside the gas tank. There was enough to get me home. I waited and then tried again.

The engine finally caught. But the Jag's jungle roar was gone. The motor sounded more like a house cat with the flu.

I feathered the throttle to turn the machine around and it barely moved. The engine had no power.

I jumped off the seat, kept my thumb on the throttle and ran alongside the sled. I turned the skis and looked off into the distance at my truck. I needed to get going. I had a lot of things to do today.

The Jag should have leaped ahead with me off the seat. But it didn't. It felt like I was pushing a cart stacked high with firewood through mud.

I was thinking, "Fouled plug? Water in the gas?" and muttering, "Come on. Come on. You can do it...."

But she couldn't. The Jag gasped, choked and the engine quit for good.

So much for saving time. I was now staring at a dead sled and facing a mile long walk over sketchy ice to get back to my truck. I had to fix this.

I flipped up the hood, found the spark plug wrench, pulled the rubber sockets on both plugs and unscrewed them.  I held them up to the sky.

The first plug was passable.  But the second was sporting a shiny silver cap.

I had torn into lots of engines.  Even repaired some.  I knew this melted metal on the plug was a bad sign.

I stuck my eyeball down against the cylinder like a heart surgeon looking inside a patient's chest for a lost sponge.

And there it was—not a sponge, but a hole the size of a dime in the top of the piston.  I'd let the motor get so hot I had melted the darn thing.  I was not going anywhere.

I looked around me more carefully.  No roads.  To tow my machine, someone would have to ride over the same weakening ice and pull the Jag back to the access area.

The result would probably be two fried snowmobile engines.  Maybe even one or two wardens in the lake.  Worst of all?  Someone might see me broken down and broadcast it.  Ouch.  That would really hurt my pride.

It was very clear the Jag was not going to move. I was going to have to hike out and radio for help.

"But isn't there some other way?" I asked myself. The way some people fear the dentist or traveling by plane is how I felt about asking for help.

"If I was home I could tear into this thing and probably fix it myself in a few hours," I thought. "How hard could it be?"

Then I remembered there was a generous parts stash stored at the Sandbar Refuge about 35 miles away. I had a key to the building.

If I could find the parts, maybe I could fix this engine right out here. I wouldn't have to ask anyone for help. No one would know. Oh, I'd tell my boss what I had done, but I'd wait until I had the Jag running again. I could fix this machine, not ask for a tow, not ask anyone for help. It would just take a little effort.

I took out my pencil and paper and made a list of what I figured I would need to rebuild the snowmobile cylinder.

Then I dropped the hood and took the key—not that anyone was going to drive the Jag away—

untied my snowshoes from the back of the sled, put them on and sloshed my way through the weeds along the shoreline to my truck.

Once back inside my truck, I headed straight to the Sandbar Refuge. I opened the door to the parts room with my key, turned on the lights, pulled out my list and started digging through the shelves.

Within 45 minutes I found a new cylinder, a piston, wrist pin and rings. I even found a set of new gaskets.

I tipped my hat to whoever had ordered all these parts. Everything I needed was there. I placed it all in a cardboard box, loaded it into my truck and headed home to my toolbox.

Early the next morning, I drove back to Lake Carmi and hiked to the sled carrying a plastic pail of parts and tools. There were sockets and box wrenches, a propane torch, a hammer and screwdrivers.

Funny thing was, the weather had completely changed. Winter was back. It was cold, with spitting snow and gusts of wind that cut right through you. The low temperature was good news if I could get the Jag going again. But it was bad news for a bush mechanic planning to rebuild a cylinder on the lake.

It didn't take me but 100 yards of walking before I stopped to tie my Elmer Fudd hat over my ears. I briefly considered turning back and calling for a tow.

But when I did, up popped a memory of my first days on the job.

I was a green recruit at a "let's all get to know one another" session. The new guys were trying to act nonchalant and mingle with wardens who had been with the department 15, 20 and even 30 years.

A senior warden approached me with a big smile and, to be polite, he handed me a mug of black coffee. He was a good foot taller than me with broad shoulders, graying hair and steel blue eyes.

I thanked him, then shifted a bit, looking around and past him to a table, first to the right and then left. He raised his eyebrows and said, "Looking for something?"

"Uh. Yes," I said, hesitating a little. I didn't want to be impolite. "Uh...Is there any half and half? Sugar?" I asked, looking up at him and smiling.

I never drank my coffee black. Made me
shudder a bit just thinking about it. It always
seemed the equivalent of downing hot used
motor oil.

The senior member of the Department looked
down his nose at me with a look that would
make a friendly baby scream.

"Well, geez, Nancy," he said, glowering at me
from beneath the brim of his big hat. "Let me
look for you."

He turned slowly to the right in an exaggerated
manner of concern, then to his left. His feet
never moved. I felt my face flush red. My eyes
shot down to inspect my boot laces.

Then he turned back towards me and growled
tersely, "No," and walked away.

And right then and there, I learned to drink
my coffee black. Because I really, really, really
wanted to be a game warden.

So, ask for help? Oh my, I don't think so.
Not if there was any other way.

The storm over Lake Carmi was picking up
and my face was pelted with ice when it wasn't

slapped by alder stems. Now and again, my
bucket of parts and tools would snag on some
brush and I would have to wrestle it free.

I reached the Jag, put down my bucket, lifted
up the hood and turned to look for a wrench.
The wind slammed the cowl shut, barely
missing my fingers.

I shook my head, turned my back to the wind,
removed the hood and set it far enough away
where I wouldn't trip on it.

But by the time I was ready to twist a wrench
on the second cylinder head bolt, I might as well
have been holding the tool between my toes.
My mittens were too clumsy for me to get a good
grip, to bust the bolts loose, even after heating
them with the propane torch.

I had no choice but to take my mittens off,
muckle onto the cold steel wrench handle with
my bare hands, kneel in the snow and give it all
I had to free it.

I told myself if this stuff were easy, everyone
would be rebuilding snowmobile engines
outdoors. Snowmobile mechanics working inside
nice warm repair shops would be out of work.

After 25 minutes of twisting, bashing and wrestling, I had eight bloody knuckles and was finally ready to pull the ruined piston.

Trouble was, I had no feeling left in my hands. They were like wooden blocks at the end of my wrists. I knew I needed to get heat on my hands fast.

So—please, don't try this at home or anywhere else—I sat down on the plastic bucket and put the propane torch between my knees.

With the igniter in one hand, I opened the gas valve clumsily, turned my shoulder so my back would be against the wind, hit the spark and prayed for the thing to light.

It took a half dozen tries, but the torch finally cooperated and sent a narrow beam of blue and orange fire shooting out.

I held my hands out in front of the flame and ran them back and forth like a chef putting the crunchy crust on a tasty crème brûlée.

I watched and sniffed for any sign of burning flesh, because my fingers were frozen. I couldn't feel a thing.

As soon as I could feel tingling in a few digits, I shut off the torch and stuck my hands under my armpits, stood and jigged up and down to get my blood moving.

Bloody knuckles, greasy digits, I didn't care. I just needed to be able to hold the new piston, rings and the gaskets when I picked them up.

I am not going to tell you rebuilding that cylinder went smoothly. Oh no. It was ugly. I dropped parts in the snow. The wind grabbed the gaskets right out of my hands once.

What I will say is—despite the wind and cold and wanting to quit a few times—I managed to put new parts in the Jag and get it roaring again.

And later that same day, I rode the Jag back along the shoreline to my truck—the smile on my face bigger than ever—despite a serious crick in my back.

The Lake Carmi rebuild lasted me four more winters of hard—but not foolhardy—winter patrols.

My "You broke it, You fix it" effort taught me to ride a little smarter than I had before.

Yes, game wardens would do just about anything to avoid admitting they needed help, if there was the slightest chance their predicament would become public knowledge.

I still hate asking for help.

However, retirement has changed me a little. Take coffee, for instance.

While, you will never hear me order a triple mocha soy sushi hummus latte topped with cinnamon, I admit it is a true pleasure to drink coffee with cream and sugar again.

Here's to you, Nancy.

But there was something else, something strange. In the bright glow of the flashlight it looked like it was beginning to snow inside the car.

# Snow Globe

CONTRIBUTED BY KEN DENTON

G ame limits meant nothing to Ned, nor did the season. We'd chased and cited him a number of times. He'd been fined, even spent a few nights in jail.

It didn't seem to make much of an impression on him.

He wasn't one of the guys who had a few beers to get his courage up and his ethics down to ready him for night hunting.

Nope, Ned put some real thought and effort into his nocturnal prowls. He worked at it.

We caught him one night shining a high rise searchlight. The contraption stood a couple feet above his car's roof. It was pretty ingenious. There was a handle that allowed him to turn the light back and forth from one side of the road to the other while driving.

Maybe he got the idea from the spotlights mounted on a lot of police cars. Or maybe he saw one of those swing arm, architect style lights that move this way and that, poised above a big drafting table.

However he came up with his Rube Goldberg contraption, it was clear Ned had spent a good bit of time and effort putting his illegal spotlight together.

He'd made it out of white metal, probably gleaned from washer and dryer bodies, and held together with some used bolts and a bit of duct tape.

From a poacher's perspective, it was a great invention. It put the light up and over the low, thick brush. Ned's periscope definitely made it easier to see deer.

But Ned had not thought this through. How was he going to explain his contraption to a game warden when he was caught riding the roads at 2 a.m. with it tied to the top of his car?

Of course, it didn't help that when we stopped him, Ned had a loaded rifle in his lap. We confiscated his prototype periscope and his gun. And Ned went back to court once again.

For a while, we didn't see or hear much from him.

He remained on my radar, but—ever the optimist—I really hoped Ned had changed his ways.

Not quite.

Two years later, the fellows and I had set up a sweet temptation for night hunters.

We placed a remote controlled buck with a six point rack on the edge of a meadow. If a vehicle came around the bend, its headlights would shine on the decoy—every driver would see the deer.

Most people would just be thankful the buck wasn't crossing the road in front of them, where they might hit it with their car. They would drive on. A few might stop, admire the animal for a few seconds, and then go on their way.

But a night hunter would see this decoy, hit the brakes, keep the deer in his headlights, grab a rifle and shoot.

We'd advanced from placing a motionless decoy out in a meadow and counting on a trigger happy fellow to grab his gun, aim fast and shoot without thinking things over.

The same remote control devices that worked for gamers in front of their TV, worked for us out in the woods. A fellow hidden in the bushes could remotely move the deer's head, even waggle the tail.

It was a lot like slowly jigging your fishing pole off the end of the dock to entice the panfish to bite. Poachers couldn't resist.

This particular night, our decoy was set up in a farm field we knew was popular with night hunters. Several men were hidden in strategic locations on both sides of the road. They were poised to nab any poacher whether his vehicle was headed east or west.

We even had Deputy Dave Stevenson parked tight to a big old farm barn, across from our decoy, in the inky shadows.

Dave had the widest view of the road and our mechanical deer.

Connected to us by radio, he could tell us when a driver was coming down the road, if they were driving a car or a truck and more.

If a night hunter pulled into the field, Dave could give chase in his truck and was ready for a foot race too.

We figured we had everything covered. I got everyone into position, made certain we were connected by radio and settled in.

Cars rolled by but no one stoped. An hour passed. Then two.

The night air was heavy and the cold seeped into our bones as we waited.

It was around 1 a.m. when Dave's voice came over the walkie talkie, hushed but anxious.

"I hear something," he said.

My back straightened. I turned my head right, then left, listening hard. I was down the road in the bushes, a long ways from Dave.

I listened for the sound of gravel turning under car tires, to see the glow from a car's dash lights, maybe moonlight reflected off a windshield.

In a few seconds, Dave's whisper again broke the night silence. "It's getting louder. I think it's coming right at me. From over the hill."

I gritted my teeth and shook my head and my mind said, "Nooooo. Are you kidding me?" This wasn't supposed to happen.

Was some farmer about to crash through the middle of our operation while searching for a stray heifer at 2 a.m.?

Was this some Romeo romancing his Juliet off in a meadow to keep the tryst hidden from prying eyes? Or was this a poacher headed towards Dave and we had set ourselves up all wrong?

If a driver topped that hill, they couldn't help but see Dave's truck next to the barn.

"It's getting closer, coming right for me," I heard Dave say. "My cover is about to be blown."

I heard it now too. It sounded like a car lugging along in first gear. But I was too far away to see anything. I held my breath and waited for Dave to tell us what was going on.

"I see it! It's a car. The headlights are off," he told us. "He's going slow, getting closer. I don't think he sees me yet. Closer..."

There was a two second pause and then Dave's slow whisper became an eardrum splitting shout. "He's spotted me. He's gunning it. I'm in pursuit! I'm in pursuit!" he yelped.

I jumped up out of my hiding place, reached out like a swimmer doing the breaststroke and parted the brush in front of me. I took a big step over the road ditch and I raced towards the meadow.

It wasn't unusual for a poacher to ditch their car and make a run for it. If that happened, I wanted to join the chase.

I saw Dave's truck headlights shining, his blue lights flashing, and the truck bucking across the big field at a teeth rattling rate.

The car he was chasing kept its headlights off. It turned right, then left. The driver was like a wily calf trying to escape a young reining horse.

The fellow driving the car made a wide turn and then gunned it back down the field road, out of my sight. No way could I catch him.

This was Dave's collar. I didn't rush to offer assistance unless he asked for it. I got the story later. Dave told me he chased that car for more than a mile before the driver finally gave up, pulled over and stopped.

By that time, both vehicles had taken some serious pounding. Dave and Ned had slammed into potholes and felt their teeth chatter as their vehicles slid across washboard roads.

When Dave jumped out of his truck, he ran up to the driver's door and yanked it open. There, he found himself looking at a familiar face.

It was our old friend, Ned, blinking hard, hands high and tight on the wheel where Dave could see them.

But there was something else, something strange. In the bright glow of the flashlight it looked like it was beginning to snow inside Ned's car.

Dave asked Ned where he was going. Ned replied he was just out for a ride. He denied he was out looking for deer.

And why did he run? Well, Ned claimed, he didn't know who or what was behind him. When he realized it was law enforcement, he stopped.

There was a light breeze this night. With the car door open and Dave talking to Ned, little bits of snow kept rising, falling and swirling around inside the car.

It was like Ned was driving a snow globe and he had shaken the thing up battering it over field stubble and rough back roads. It wasn't unusual for dust and pollen to float around a car after a good shaking, but this snow didn't want to quit.

Little bits of white caught the breeze and floated up and down. As Ned continued his story, Dave noticed a snowflake drift down from the roof liner. It landed on Ned's collar. It didn't melt.

Dave leaned in an inch or so and stared harder at it. It wasn't a snowflake at all. It was a tiny white feather.

Dave turned his light a few degrees to the left and there on the dash were more little flecks of white, gliding across the dash like the parachute seeds of dandelions.

Dave turned his light towards the backseat of Ned's car. On the floor was a worn green wool Army blanket and what appeared to be the nose of a 12 gauge shotgun poking out.

"Okay, Ned," Dave said. "How about you step out of the car nice and easy with your hands up high where I can see them?"

Ned grumbled, but did as he was told. Dave had Ned put his palms flat on the hood. Then Dave opened the back door of the car and shined his light.

Dave stood away from the shotgun barrel and slowly peeled back the blanket. There, he found the source of the "It's beginning to look a lot like Christmas" feeling inside Ned's car.

Ned had stashed 17 grouse on the floor of his car. It was clear he'd had an exceptional day hunting the popular game fowl. Ned was about four times over the legal limit.

As Dave counted the birds, he saw Ned had begun to pluck some of them.

That partial plucking, along with having driven his car the way James Bond likes his martinis—shaken, not stirred—had given the dead birds the opportunity to tattle on Ned.

We surmised Ned decided he was on a hot streak and he had come into the meadow with his headlights off with the intention of taking a deer home too.

Dave searched the car and found a deer rifle in the vehicle. But it was not loaded.

We did not have enough evidence to cite Ned for attempting to poach deer.

Not this time anyway. But the feathers got him.

Ned drove home with a citation for possessing too many grouse. The birds went into a pouch and it went into the back of Dave's truck. Dave wanted to avoid a repeat snow globe phenomenon inside his vehicle.

Dave and I knew Ned was likely to see grouse feathers wafting around his vehicle for a long time—maybe years—thanks to his attempt to outrun the law. Little things tend to fall into corners and then come popping up when you least expect them.

And we knew, whenever Ned saw a tiny feather dance across his car dash or settle onto the passenger seat beside him, he would recall forfeiting all those grouse—and game wardens.

It's so nice to be remembered, isn't it?

*"INCOMING!" my mind*
*shouted as if I was in a war.*
*"RUN!" Walt and I both yelled*
*across the ice.*

# SHANTY SURPRISE

CONTRIBUTED BY KEN DENTON & WALT ACKERMANN

C ome the end of ice fishing season, wardens need to check lakes and ponds for shanties the owners have failed to remove from state waters.

The state has a deadline and Mother Nature has one too. And while they aren't always coordinated, common sense will tell you it is a good idea to get your shack off the pond before your kids are asking for tanning oil and flip flops.

But trucks break down, people get busy or just procrastinate. There's a ton of reasons why people fail to get their shanties off the ice before what we call "Break Up."

That leaves wardens to take the risk— hopefully, not the plunge—for the owners. But procrastination has a price. Ice fishermen who miss the state's deadline can find themselves with a citation and a fine.

That's the situation Deputies Walt Ackermann, Dave Stevenson and I faced one March evening on Keiser Pond in Danville.

The three of us planned on checking the smelt run a few miles away once it got dark.

But I had visited Keiser a few days earlier and spotted one shanty sitting out there all alone.

Moving a big shanty to shore was a job for two or three people and a truck with good tires on solid winter ice.

Now, with the ice melting— thanks to a stretch of warm, sunny days—I wondered if getting this beast off the ice and onto the shore would even be possible.

To leave the sheds to drop into the water is not just thoughtless, but dangerous.

Water currents break the plywood and lumber into bobbing bombs. Complete with nails, the discarded lumber can easily rip a hole in the bottom of a boat, slam and break a propeller,

foul shorelines and spike the feet of camp
owners trying to put in their dock or just go
for a swim months later. Chemicals in the
paint and plywood, along with rusting metal
roofing and nails create more hazards for fish
and other aquatic life.

I had called Dave and Walt earlier in the day,
and asked them to meet me at the pond's
access area. If we were lucky, the owner would
have taken the shack away.

But if the shed was still on the ice, the job was
ours. The weather forecast this week promised
rising temperatures. The shanty would crash
through the ice soon.

Pulling in a half hour before sunset, there it
was—an immobile Moby Dick. I felt a twinge
of Captain Ahab in me as I squinted out over
the ice to assess the challenge.

It was a crudely built 10 x 12 plywood
testament to the sport of ice fishing. Just four
walls, a mix of rough lumber and plywood.
The roof was rusting sheet metal.

The shanty had two windows, if you could
call them that. They were nothing more than

rough holes, probably cut freehand with a jigsaw, then covered in plastic. The front door was tongue and groove painted red, which had faded to a strange pink. The shack sat on a pair of wooden skids built out of 2 x 4s that didn't look strong enough to support it.

Despite its shortcomings, I knew the shack was a welcome hideout on frigid days. Get inside, drill a few holes in the ice, flip your five gallon pail over, bait your hook and dip your pole. Invite in some friends. A lot of guys love jigging for fish and just listening to the wind howl outside.

But standing on the shore that early Spring evening, I was more than a little concerned. Walt, Dave or I could end up in the icy water before we got the shanty to shore.

It looked to me like maybe the skids had sunk a couple inches into the ice.

Walt and Dave arrived and jumped out of their truck and walked down to stand at the shoreline beside me.

I gave them a minute to study the job, and then asked, "What do you think, Gentlemen?"

Walt's head was high evaluating the enemy, his chin jutted out. His eyes were thin slits due to the late day glare of the sun.

It struck me that, at this particular moment, Walt bore a striking resemblance to General Douglas MacArthur. If he'd pulled a corncob pipe out of his pocket and clenched it between his teeth it would not have surprised me one bit.

"Won't take long," Walt said with a sniff and nonchalant confidence. "I'll get my rope."

Walt was my go to guy when it came to towing, hauling, tying stuff down—anything to do with rope. Skimp was not in his vocabulary.

There were plenty of small town hardware stores with less line in stock than Walt carried with him. He had a particular fondness for ¾ inch wide, yellow braided nylon. And he had a lot of it. Hundreds of feet of the stuff.

You could have circled a dozen cows with it, cinched them up together and with a bucket of grain rustled the entire herd without calling in any cow ponies.

"Yeah. We can do it," Dave agreed. "No problem."

I had a lot of respect for both men. Walt had worked every job imaginable on his family's dairy farm.

He had hogtied and hauled everything from stuck manure spreaders to irate cows through waist deep mud and across dodgy ice.

Dave worked on the road crew for the Town of Barnet. He was the guy to have with you when it came to car and truck mechanics.

I looked at the pressure cracks in the ice, the pools of water bubbling up along deep surface cracks and shook my head.

"We're sure not walking out there," I sighed.

"I'll untie the canoe," Dave replied. He turned to walk back to the truck where it was tied in the bed.

"It'll be dark soon," I noted, walking beside Dave to help him. "We've got to hustle."

Dave and I pulled the aluminum canoe out of the truck bed, placed two paddles and life vests inside and carried it to the edge of the pond ice.

Walt poked one arm through his giant coiled
hank of rope, kneeled low and tied it to the
truck's tow hitch and bumper.

Then he played the line out to the canoe and
dropped the rest in a neat coil on the canoe
floor up near the bow.

Walt and I grabbed our life vests, zipped them
up and looked at one another.

"You might as well take the bow, Walt. It's your
rope," I said. Walt nodded and together we
pushed the nose of the canoe out onto the ice
and he stepped inside gently.

I pushed the stern until we were all the way
on the ice, got myself balanced to counter my
partner's weight and said, "Okay. Let's try it."

The job required each man to be half in and
half out of the canoe—one in the stern leaning
off the port side and the other in the bow
leaning to starboard—you counterbalance the
other person.

Think of a centipede, which has met with a
series of very unfortunate accidents but refuses
to quit.

You would keep your outside leg out over the ice, your boot pushing the canoe forward. You used your paddle just to help you keep the boat upright.

It's critical to coordinate your movement with the other person and pay attention. Make a wrong move and you could flip the canoe and both end up in ice water—or worse, get sucked beneath the ice by strong currents.

The canoe helps spread the weight and gives you something to reach for if you do break through and fall in—it would float if we turned turtle.

Dave stayed on shore, prepared to act if the canoe dumped us. He would drive his truck to tow the shanty.

It took some careful coordination to get out there, over the peaks of cracked ice and through sloshing ice water.

When we got to within 20 feet of the shanty I asked Walt how he was going to tackle the job.

"I'm gonna swing to the right and make a loop around the top of those skids and the lower half of the shanty as best I can," he said. "If we can get the rope around it a couple of times that would be good. Then I'll tie it off and we'll head back."

"All right, I'll follow your lead," I said. "Just let me know what you're doing before you do it. Take it slow and steady."

"Right," Walt said. "I don't want to get too close to the shanty. If it breaks through the ice, we could go with it."

Water topped the shanty's doubled 2 x 4 skids in some spots. I couldn't tell if the shed was still frozen tight to the ice or ready to pop free and slide with a light pull.

We pushed the canoe around the shanty once, and Walt pulled the rope tight just above the skids.

Then we went around the building again, coursing the line a few feet higher up the walls, just to be certain the truck would have a good hold on it when Dave drove ahead.

When Walt was done, he made a few big hitches in the line, so it would snug up on the shanty when Dave pulled. By the time we turned the bow to head to shore, I could no longer see Dave, just his flashlight beam back on the shore, guiding us in.

"I can barely see you. Let's get off this ice quick," I urged Walt.

"Gotcha," Walt agreed.

I breathed a sigh of relief when Walt and I put our boots on solid ground.

We picked the canoe up and carried it onto the shore about 20 feet from where we figured the shanty would be coming in, then turned towards Dave.

"Okay, Dave, I guess you're up," I said, giving him the go ahead to tow. "Keep your window open so you can hear us? And just take it slow. We'll yell if there's a problem."

Dave nodded, jumped behind the wheel, turned on his headlights and aimed a big spotlight on the side of his truck towards the ice, so we could all watch the shack's progress into shore.

Dave began the slow pull, driving up the access road. It wasn't a straight run. He had to turn and go up a small hill.

Walt and I stood at the edge of the shore, ready to grab the shanty, to muscle it the final few feet from the ice.

It was pitch black out. Our only light came from the truck, spotlighting the shanty like a Broadway stage.

Walt and I stood. Silent.

Dave drove 50 feet, then 80, then 110 feet up the access road. It didn't seem to make a difference. The nylon stretched, but the shanty didn't budge.

I was thinking, "Any second now, I'll see the shanty shudder. Those skids will break out of the ice."

But it was like Dave was pulling salt water taffy in a seashore shop in Maine. Nothing happened. I looked over at Walt. "Nylon stretches," he said and shrugged. I turned, looked up the road for Dave.

My jaw dropped when I saw how far away he was—at least 150 feet, headed around a bend. The shanty still sat out on the ice where we'd left it. The shack hadn't budged. The bright light of his spotlight had dimmed a bit, he was so far away from us.

"Something's gotta give. How much more tension can that rope take?" I said to myself. I cocked my head, squinted, stared at the skids. When they moved, the building would move.

That's when I saw the shanty lift straight up into the air, six feet above the ice, and disappear. Poof. Gone.

There was nothing but a pool of water where the shanty's skids had sat. It was as if a magician had snapped his fingers and made the big shack vanish.

My mouth fell open. I looked at the pond in disbelief. It was a "Now you see it, now you don't" event. I wouldn't have been surprised to hear an orchestra strike up a "TA DA!" and a grinning man wearing a top hat and a red lined, satin cape step into the spotlight and take a bow.

Where did it go?  I peered into the dark.
I listened hard.  I knew Walt was doing the
same.  We didn't speak.  Our minds were
trying to process what our eyes had seen.

Two seconds later, I heard whistling sounds
and a series of whooshes cutting the air.

I stood still, trying to place the sound.
A backyard rocket fired into the night sky
came to mind.

My brain worked to comprehend what I had
just witnessed.  The shanty was out on the
ice 125 feet away from us.  We circled it with
rope and Dave was trying to pull it to shore.
And now it's gone—all gone.  And now there's
whooshes getting louder and...  I got it.

"INCOMING!" my mind shouted as if I was in
a war.  "RUN!"  Walt and I both yelled at once.
We turned and ran for cover.

The shanty had exploded.

The combination of the truck pulling the rope
noose tighter and the pond ice holding the
shanty skids fast, had caused the shack to
blow apart.

Splintered boards, nails, plywood, rusty tin—all were in the air somewhere and headed for us.

Equally bad, I knew Walt's nylon rope was traveling at something like a gazillion miles an hour towards Dave's bumper, trying to catch up with itself—right between the two of us. If that line struck either one of us, it would cut deep, could even decapitate us.

I wished for snow banks—something Walt and I could dive behind, take cover. It was run, dive, get low and pray time.

Dave felt the release of pressure on the truck's engine and heard our yells. He braked, looked back and saw Walt and me running like a bear was chasing us.

I heard Dave yell, "You guys all right down there?"

Good question. I was wondering that myself.

It was times like this when I was reluctant to take a hard look at myself for fear I'd find a splintered 2 x 4 sticking out of my arm, leg, gut or head. You'd just rather not know, you know?

I took a deep breath, then picked myself up off the mix of snow, ice and gravel, stood up and turned to look for Walt. I found him 10 feet away, getting back onto his feet. We quietly checked one another out.

When it was clear we were both still intact, no major blood loss, we nodded at one another, smiled and took a deep breath.

I turned and yelled up to Dave. "Yeah. We're okay. Rope must have snapped."

Dave jumped out of his truck, quickly coiled and tossed the huge wad of yellow line into the truck bed and then backed the truck down to where we stood.

He angled the spotlight to help us look for the shanty—or what had been the shanty.

It was as if I'd held a deck of cards over my head and turned them loose in a hurricane. Pieces were scattered over the ice in a swath 30 feet wide and 50 feet long. Smaller bits had landed just a few feet from where Walt and I had been standing.

We'd been lucky.

The work order changed from towing to pick up sticks. We still had to get that shanty gone, even if it was in pieces. Our plan to check the smelt run? It disappeared with the shanty.

After some brief "Do you believe this just happened?" discussion, the three of us got back down to business.

Walt and I picked up the canoe. Dave handed us a shorter rope and a rake.

We made several trips back out over the ice, roping busted roofing and boards and plywood and then tossing the rope to Dave so he could tow the pile onto shore. Some pieces we placed in the bottom of the canoe and ferried in.

We returned the next morning to finish the job. That's when we found chunks of metal roofing, the door and broken boards scattered about like a tiny tornado had touched down. It took us hours to clean the mess up and haul it away.

I paid the fellow who owned the shack a visit a few days later. I gave him a citation for failing to remove it, along with the grim news he would never see his ice shanty again.

I can't say he was heartbroken.

As for the fine he paid for abandoning the shack? I doubt it covered the real cost of the three of us getting it off the ice.

And what about wardens having to risk their necks?

But 20 plus years later, when Walt and Dave and I get together and recall our best adventures, the Keiser Pond Shanty Show is always mentioned.

It was as good a magic act as you'll ever see.

Best of all, we lived.

*Doug liked to trade booze for tips on where trophy bucks could be found. He'd use his most trusted bar patrons to help him find, kill and transport them.*

# DOUG'S DEN

CONTRIBUTED BY NORM BROWN

**T**rying to nab Doug was like lying in a snowbank at midnight trying to tighten a leaking oil filter with your bare hands.

Slippery and frustrating.

Rumors of Doug's poaching had circulated for years. We spent hundreds of hours on his trail and came close to catching him red handed several times. But, time and again, he slipped through our hands.

It took a shocking call from a Maine warden, a gutsy Vermont deputy warden putting the pieces together at his day job, a terrified taxidermist and the zeal and resources of federal prosecutors to deep six Doug.

Give the devil his due—Doug created a sophisticated poaching operation worthy of a big city crime syndicate. And when I think back on those days, that analogy might be close to the truth of what he was doing in our little valley.

Like me, Doug lived in Vermont, along the New York state border. The Mettawee River meanders through the region, providing a welcome haven for all kinds of wildlife.

The area features lovely farms, a proud history of slate quarrying, good hunting and a great quality of life.

Doug was one of us. He grew up here, joined the military and served in Viet Nam. And when he returned from the war he opened a bar he called Doug's Den on Water Street in neighboring Granville, New York—just across the state line from Wells, Vermont.

Granville had a bigger population to draw from and the bars could stay open longer than in Vermont.

More a dark alley than a road, Water Street was where fights, drinking and drug dealing were likely after dark.

You'd see lots of banged up pickup trucks —with drivers to match—turn down that lane, from early afternoon on into the wee hours.

Even police didn't like to go into Water Street after dark.

But it didn't bother Doug. He was admired by patrons for being a smart local guy who ran his own business.

Doug's Den was known for the hunting trophies hanging on the walls. Doug had a thing for antlers. He wanted the biggest whitetails with the biggest racks.

And he didn't care how he got them.

With many of the pub's patrons out of work due to a precipitous decline in the region's 100 year old slate industry, cold hard cash was hard to come by.

Doug was one of many who turned to bartering rather than demand cash. As a bar owner, he was in the catbird seat. He could swap drinks for favors. He could even water

down the drinks if he thought he had paid
too much.

The stories that came to us said Doug liked to
trade booze for tips on where trophy bucks could
be found.  He'd use his most trusted bar patrons
to help him find, kill and transport them.

Over time, Doug's Den became a nerve center
for poaching.

An area slaughterhouse that processed cows
and sheep during the day would slide in deer
from Doug's Den at night.  Those deer didn't
need to be trophies.  Meat cutters would wrap
and sell the venison to restaurants down the
road in Albany or as far as New York City.

New York law enforcement heard many
of the same rumors my deputies and I did.
But catching Doug was the challenge.

He had loyal lookouts everywhere.

Making things more complicated was the
jurisdictional issue.  The fish and game laws in
New York were, and still are, different than in
Vermont.  Enforcement differed too.

Doug kept my deputies and me on high alert many nights.

The guys working as deputies with me during this time were: Doug Bishop of Poultney, John Colvin of Middletown Springs, Terry Williams of Poultney and Dave Keeler of Danby. I knew I could call on any one of these men and they would back me up 100 percent.

I'd hand picked these fellows for their intelligence, commitment, ability to deal with the public and willingness to arrest their mother if they believed she had violated the law.

Trouble was, if we chased Doug in Vermont and he slipped over the border into New York, our hands were tied. Vermont wardens had no legal authority there.

Sure, I could radio my New York counterpart. But by the time we coordinated our efforts, Doug would have covered his tracks.

Doug surrounded himself with guys like some Mafia don. Various cronies rode shotgun with him in his truck, keeping an eye out for police or maybe guys he'd crossed.

He employed decoy shooters, staged calls to wardens in towns miles away, even had his guys changing vehicles after a night hunt. Doug organized poaching like a winning coach chooses his players.

He and his crew kept police scanners in their homes and vehicles. They listened in and worked to stay a jump or two ahead of us.

One night we got a lucky break. Someone called the police saying they had just seen a shot fired from a black truck. The caller said a passenger ran out into a meadow and came back with a dead deer over their shoulders, threw it into the truck bed, climbed back into the vehicle and sped away.

They were even able to get the license plate. When the Dispatcher read it over the scanner I felt like I held a winning lottery ticket.

It was Doug's truck. I had memorized his plate number. All of my men had.

My supervisor, Floyd Lanphere Jr., of Proctor, was home and heard the call on his scanner too. Floyd relayed a message to me that he would pick up John in Middletown Springs and the two of them would hurry over to assist.

Floyd was a deputy federal marshal as well as a Vermont warden.

If Doug intended to cross over into New York thinking that would save him, he would have to think again. Floyd could go after him.

Terry was with me in my cruiser. We searched the back roads in the area where the shot had been reported, looking for Doug's truck.

Meanwhile, Floyd and John crossed the border into New York from West Pawlet, Vermont.

Floyd spotted Doug's truck parked at a bar called Kelly's on the outskirts of Granville and quietly pulled into the lot—no blue lights, not even his cruiser headlights on.

Before the wheels had even stopped rolling, John slipped out of the passenger seat of Floyd's cruiser, stayed low and leaped into the bed of Doug's truck to search for blood and deer hair.

Within seconds, someone inside the bar spotted John shining his flashlight in the back of Doug's black pickup and sounded the alarm.

It was like Floyd and John had stepped on a hornet's nest.

A dozen guys came roaring out of the bar onto a well worn porch, ready to brawl. Doug was in the lead.

"Get outta my truck! Get outta there! You got no right," Doug bellered at Floyd and John, his right fist pumping the night air.

Floyd stepped out of the cruiser and said calmly, "Just take it easy, Doug. We've had a complaint of a deer being taken tonight and we're just following up." Floyd explained to Doug he had authority to work in New York.

Doug screamed back, "This is New York! I'm in New York! You've got no right to search here! No right!" and he took a big step like he was going to lunge off the porch and charge Floyd and John.

The bar crowd was with him. The fellows behind Doug and along the porch railing started to curse and shout at the uniformed men.

But Floyd and John had back up. Floyd had a German Shepherd cross, Lady, who didn't like it when people yelled at her master.

She leaped out of the cruiser's backseat window and came running up into the light.

The black and silver hair along her spine stood up about three inches. She growled and slinked across the pavement, just six feet from the men that threatened Floyd. Her fangs glistened in the dim street light outside the bar.

Doug and his crew stopped dead in their tracks. They might have thought they could take the two men, but none of them had counted on being attacked by a big dog.

Floyd and John knew Lady couldn't keep a dozen drunk and angry men at bay for long. Someone would throw a bottle or the entire bunch might charge them if they didn't leave soon.

John jumped down from Doug's truck bed and held his hand up—his thumb and index finger pressed together—smiled and nodded to Floyd. It was John's way of telling Floyd he had, indeed, found fresh blood and hair. The evidence was in his hand and would go into an evidence bag.

John hurried back to the cruiser.

Floyd calmed the scene down, told the bar crowd they were leaving.

He walked back a few steps and opened the cruiser's back door for Lady. She came running and jumped inside. Then Floyd slid behind the steering wheel and the trio headed down the road to find Terry and me.

We met up a mile away.

We knew Doug had to have dropped the dead deer between where it was reported killed and Kelly's. He clearly intended to wait a bit, then go get it.

We had to find it first. Where had Doug cached the carcass?

I knew Doug's sister lived on the road to Kelly's, less than a quarter mile away, on the old family farm. Doug had grown up there. As I talked out loud, we all agreed it made sense that was where he most likely hid the deer.

All four of us rushed over there. The house lights were on. I went to the door and knocked. When Doug's sister opened the door I told her we wanted to search the outbuildings and why.

She shrugged her shoulders and yawned. She didn't seem at all surprised.

"I'm tired," she said. "I've got to get some sleep, then get up and go to work in a couple of hours. You guys do whatever you want," she said and closed the front door.

I explained the situation to Floyd, John and Terry.

We agreed we still needed a search warrant. So, I jumped into my vehicle with Terry alongside me and we raced off to get one.

Floyd and John stayed at the scene, waiting and watching. I got the warrant and rushed back. I made it back to the farm in less than two hours.

It was close to 2 a.m. when the four of us were finally able to search the premises. There were two big barns and several old sheds.

We opened doors, climbed rickety ladders, crawled into haylofts and scared up a few bats.

All we found were a loose rope hanging from a rafter, a few drops of fresh blood and wisps of deer hair in a small tool shed bordering the woods beyond the abandoned cow barn.

We figured Doug had made a phone call from the pay phone at Kelly's to a guy who owed him a favor.

Someone snuck into the shed from the woods while Floyd and John waited for Terry and I to come back with the search warrant.

Doug's guys had grabbed the carcass, raced back through the woods, loaded it into a vehicle and driven away. The deer had disappeared.

We were four wardens trying to seal off and search a 100 acre farm, late at night.

Doug probably had a dozen guys to call on, to help him out. I envisioned Doug strolling over to the pay phone at Kelly's after Floyd pulled away, dialing up one of the guys who owed him a favor and asking him to sneak through the woods in back of his sister's place and get the doe out of the shed fast.

Doug would have hung up the phone grinning, knowing we would never find the evidence.

He probably didn't even have to put down his drink.

He had managed to slip through our hands once again.

It wasn't the first time. It wouldn't be the last.

*With the shuttered Hampton Manor
looking on, agents pulled their weapons
and pointed them straight at Doug.*

# DOUG'S DONE

CONTRIBUTED BY NORM BROWN

After the confrontation at Kelly's Bar, Doug realized Vermont wardens had a way to follow him into New York state. He took even more precautions.

Doug probably should have stayed in the military and planned covert operations. To give our nemesis his due, he was good.

My deputies and I stayed busy, catching our share of night shiners and poachers. But Doug? He was always just out of reach.

Years passed. The rumors about his poaching continued. All we could do was hope one day he would make a mistake.

Deputy Warden Terry Williams was working for a big manufacturer in nearby Rutland to support his growing family. Nights and weekends, he put on a uniform to help me.

Many of the hundreds of fellows at this factory were avid hunters. Terry's supervisor, Vinny, didn't hunt, but listening to all these men talk about hunting, he saw an opportunity.

Vinny knew Terry worked part time as a deputy game warden.

He mentioned to Terry he had enrolled in a mail order taxidermy course. Said he figured he could make extra money by having the hunters in the plant come to him to preserve their trophy turkeys, deer and bear.

Terry mentioned Vinny's new hobby to me in passing. I didn't think much of it, until Terry told me some weeks later Vinny talked about stuffing owls and hawks for practice.

Terry and I both knew those birds were off limits under federal law. And knowing what animals and birds you could possess should be the first thing a taxidermy student learns.

"See what else you can find out from him," I said to Terry.

A few days later, during a work break, Terry casually asked Vinny how he happened to get big birds for his new hobby. Vinny told Terry the birds were road kill or given to him by friends.

I asked my deputy to tell me more. Terry said Vinny was a guy who didn't fit well in the macho male culture inside the plant. Vinny was rail thin and so nervous his hands would shake trying to thread a bolt.

There were bullies in the plant who delighted in sneaking up on Vinny and dropping a fat shop manual or a piece of sheet metal right behind him—anything to make the guy jump and shake. They'd pretend it was an accident. They knew it would be hard to prove otherwise. And they also knew Vinny would never take a swing at them. He wanted so badly to fit in, he just let it go and tried to laugh it off.

So, when Terry listened to Vinny, appeared to be taking some interest in his new hobby and even asked him a few questions about how it was going, Vinny was thrilled.

And this put Terry in a very tough spot.

He felt bad for Vinny who just wanted a friend. But Terry was also sworn to uphold the law and that didn't stop when he walked into his day job.

Terry knew if he got Vinny in trouble, he might destroy his family's financial future. Working in this factory was one of a very few jobs in the region that paid well. Terry depended on the paycheck to pay his bills. Working as a deputy warden paid very little.

Terry had everything to lose and nothing to gain if Vinny was cited for breaking state and federal game laws. But he would know he'd done the right thing.

Terry agreed to continue to encourage Vinny to talk about his hobby and to report whatever Vinny said, back to me.

I wanted to know who was giving Vinny protected birds. Was someone shooting hawks and owls and giving them to Vinny to stuff? Was Vinny selling the birds? Who else was involved? What else was he planning to work on?

A taxidermist doesn't work alone. Guys who poach wildlife often want to memorialize their kills and for that, they would need someone like Vinny.

Ethical taxidermists would never accept the birds Vinny told Terry he was working on.

Was Vinny ignorant of the law? Or was he working on these birds knowing he should not possess them?

It didn't really matter. It was against the law. But I wanted to know more, to cast a wider net. It sounded like some factory workers were supplying illegal wildlife to Vinny. I wanted their names. Terry had to take it slow. He had to get information from Vinny without his boss ever thinking he might be falling into a trap.

So, when Terry and I got together—which was often—Terry would tell me when Vinny had shared anything new.

I wanted to know who was supplying Vinny with birds or mammals, especially if they were illegal.

It was in the Fall when the scales of justice finally tipped our way—in a way than neither Terry nor I could ever have imagined.

It was like a bright light shined down from Heaven and said, "You have great patience. Here is your reward."

Out of the blue, a Maine warden called me at home, to inquire about the registered owner of a truck bearing a Vermont license plate.

He told me a hunter in his district was deep into the Maine woods along one of that state's many unnamed trails—tote roads, they call them—when he heard a shot. The hunter jumped in his truck to look for the shooter and came upon a very fresh, and very ugly, moose kill.

Someone had shot a big bull as it stood on the edge of the tote road and left it there to rot—hundreds of pounds of meat.

All that was taken were the moose antlers and the cape—the hide of the animal from the nose to the shoulders.

The poacher had sawn the antlers off just above the animal's skull in a hurry, with what looked to be a hacksaw, my Maine colleague told me.

It was clear whoever killed the giant just wanted it for a trophy. They weren't at all interested in the meat.

The Maine warden told me the hunter who came upon the scene had spotted a black Ford truck with Vermont plates speeding away. He'd grabbed his field glasses and managed to write down the license plate number.

Then he drove to the closest phone and called Maine authorities.

It was quite a story. The Maine warden paused and asked if I knew the fellow. He told me the man's first name was Douglas...

"Yes, I know who he is," I told him. "I sure do."

And what he had just told me made perfect sense based on what I knew of Doug's obsession with antlers.

After a 50 year ban on moose hunting in Maine, authorities had agreed to a limited hunt, with a few hundred permits available to residents only.

It was big news all over the country. It was in all the hunting magazines and the talk of hunters all over New England.

Doug would be one of thousands of guys nationwide wishing he could somehow join those lucky few Mainers, with a chance to bring home a trophy moose.

Assuming the Maine warden had the truck and poacher correct, my challenge was finding the evidence. But how?

Where between northern Maine and Granville, New York, would Doug have stashed a moose antlers and hide?

It was clear he intended to have the antlers and cape mounted. That meant he would need a taxidermist fast. Antlers you can keep around, no problem. But hide doesn't keep. Animal skins require immediate attention by a professional to be properly preserved.

The taxidermy world is a small one. Get caught taking in animal parts without the correct paper trail and you face huge fines—even jail time. What taxidermist would take that risk?

When Terry went to work Monday, we found out.

Vinny came up to Terry on their break with a big smile on his face and his eyes twinkling. He was like a kid bursting to share a secret.

"Hey, guess what I got this weekend?" he whispered to Terry. "You're never gonna believe it! This guy brought me a bull moose. Huge antlers! Really nice.... "

Terry looked down at the floor. He didn't want Vinny to see his face. He just nodded.

Terry was thinking, "Why would a Mainer be bringing a moose to Vermont for Vinny to mount—a total amateur?"

Vinny paused, waiting for a reaction from Terry. Terry had to appear interested but not too interested.

"Wow. That's really something," Terry said trying to be nonchalant. "Lucky guy. Big one too, hunh? Who got it?"

"This fellow owns a bar over in Granville," Vinny said. "Quite the big game hunter, I guess. Knows some of the guys who work here. They told him about me and my new business. His name is Doug...."

Terry nodded and let Vinny brag on, hanging on every word but pretending he was just happy for Vinny.

"The only thing is, he wants this done really fast," Vinny said of his client. "He's only giving me two weeks. I really need to dry the hide. And the book says...." Vinny started going on about all the intricacies of tanning.

Terry kept his head down and nodded, pretended to listen, but his mind was racing.

For Deputy Warden Williams, it was go time.

When their break was over, Terry made an excuse, told Vinny his stomach was a little upset. He was gonna have to take a couple extra minutes and head to the restroom. Was that okay?

Vinny nodded his approval.

But instead of heading to the bathroom, Terry waited until Vinny was around the corner, then rushed to the pay phone. He made certain no one could overhear him and called me.

I listened and realized Terry had just uncovered a very big case. Could we get them? Terry said Doug expected the mount in less than two weeks. How were we ever going to get Doug in such a short amount of time?

I had an idea. But it was going to require a lot more manpower.

Having killed and transported moose parts across state lines, Doug had violated the Lacey Act, a federal law designed to stop exactly this kind of crime. The Lacey Act provides big fines and jail time for anyone trafficking in illegal animal parts.

As soon as I got off the phone with Terry, I called Floyd. With his deputy federal marshal hat, as well as his Vermont game warden status, I knew Floyd would be our best advocate.

Again, luck was on our side. One of Vermont's federal prosecutors was an avid birder. Where a lot of attorneys ranked crimes against wildlife far below those against people, this gentleman was with us 100 percent.

We were told, whatever resources we needed, we'd get. He wasn't kidding.

Federal marshals, wire taps, air surveillance out of the Rutland airport to follow Doug's truck as he drove back and forth to meet with Vinny— that was part of it. We had people on board like you wouldn't believe.

It was time to lower the boom on Vinny. To get Doug, we needed Vinny to talk.

Terry had told me Vinny was a nervous guy, but few can imagine the level of anxiety he had.

When I confronted him—me dressed in my uniform and with federal agents present too— and we told him the years in jail and thousands of dollars in fines he was facing for taking in protected species, I thought he was going to pass out.

His eyes went back into his head and his hands fluttered up off the chair arms. His feet shuffled on the linoleum like he was a trying to dig a hole in the ground and climb inside it.

Vinny was a shaky, sweaty, stammering mess. He made Barney Fife of Mayberry seem like James Bond. Several times I thought he would slide out of the chair onto the floor like a lonely strand of cooked spaghetti.

Vinny had to work with us, so we could get the evidence to prove it was Doug who shot the moose, Doug who transported the antlers and hide across state borders, Doug who brought the moose to Vermont to be mounted.

We knew Doug had just met Vinny and didn't know him well. We figured Doug had been told by his pals that Vinny was an odd, nervous type.

But we believed if Vinny sweated profusely, couldn't make eye contact, stammered and searched for words, Doug would bolt. Maybe he would send a pal to pick up the mount, but he would be too smart to do it himself.

We wanted Doug on tape admitting he killed the moose and transported the antlers and cape across state lines. And for that, we needed Vinny to chat him up on the phone and in person, to get Doug to relax, maybe talk about finding and killing the bull in Maine, cutting it up and hauling the antlers to Vinny.

We told Vinny if he helped us get Doug, we would go easier on him. Eventually, he agreed.

But when we gave him the specifics—his phone calls would be recorded, he would wear a wire and be coached on what to say—Vinny gasped and gulped air like a goldfish that had jumped out of its bowl.

First and foremost, we needed Vinny to stick to his daily routine. That meant going to work every day, talking to the same people, acting like nothing was out of the ordinary.

But the very next day, before noon, he called to say he couldn't sleep, he couldn't eat and his stomach was killing him.

If Doug's pals at the factory believed Vinny was acting even more anxious than usual, they might tell Doug.

Doug relied on his instincts. If he thought anything at all was off, he'd bolt like a thirsty mustang that had seen a cougar at the same watering hole 10 years earlier.

Within two days it became clear we were going to lose Vinny to a hospital bed or maybe even a funeral parlor. He said he couldn't eat. He was losing weight. He felt dizzy a lot.

We realized there was no way Vinny was going to last two weeks, when the taxidermist and the poacher had agreed Doug would pick up his trophy.

We had to come up with a way to get Doug to come to Vinny's house, to talk about the moose, to prove his involvement, before Vinny collapsed.

Federal agents rehearsed with Vinny, like they were getting him ready for a starring role on Broadway.

Fingers crossed, we had Vinny call Doug and ask him to come over and look at the stitching Vinny had done on the cape, to make certain it was satisfactory. "I want you to take a look before I finish the job," Vinny told him. "When can you come over?"

Vinny's hands shook so bad making the call,
we thought he would drop the phone. When he
reached for a glass of water it spilled all down
his shirt and onto the floor.

But Vinny's call worked. Doug agreed to come
over the next day at 10 a.m.

Agents were in the woods out back of
Vinny's, watching for Doug. Vinny was wired.
We waited.

Doug drove the 40 miles from Granville to
Shrewsbury, drove by Vinny's house real slow
and... He kept going.

For whatever reason, Doug didn't pull into the
driveway.

Something had spooked him. But what? Did
he see someone or something? Had the entire
operation been blown?

We had no idea.

The only thing we knew for certain was that
the longer this operation went on, the greater
the chance we would lose our informant—
Vinny—to a nervous breakdown or some other
health issue. The thin man had lost almost

nine pounds in three days. His skin color was dirty putty.

If Vinny missed work or ended up in the hospital before the scheduled rendezvous, Doug would hear about it. Doug was no dummy. He would smell trouble and disappear.

As bad as Doug wanted that big bull's antlers hanging on his bar wall, he'd walk away rather than risk getting caught.

So, two days later, we had Vinny call Doug and tell him he had worked all night on the thing. The mount was ready. He could come pick it up.

Once again, we worked hours rehearsing the lines with Vinny, trying to get him to sound relaxed and upbeat on the phone—no alarm, nothing unusual, in his voice.

The stitching concern? We had him say, "I took care of it. I think it all looks real good. You're gonna like it a lot."

Agents put a wire on Vinny as he made the phone call. The hope was that we could record Doug saying something like, "Great. I'll be right over to get my moose."

But Vinny was so sweaty and he shook so
bad, the tape holding the wire peeled right off
his skin, fell and landed in a wet wad atop his
BVDs. Vinny's conversation with Doug never
made it onto tape.

Still, agents heard Doug tell Vinny he would
stop by around 10 a.m. the following morning
to pick up the trophy.

Federal and state law enforcement worked
through the night to coordinate people
and vehicles. This case had the U.S. Fish
and Wildlife Service, the Federal Bureau of
Investigation and game wardens from Maine,
Vermont and New York all working on it.

The plan was for officers to be hidden in
the yard, another wire placed on Vinny and
more agents inside the house, listening and
watching.

There was a plane at the Rutland airport
ready to track Doug from overhead. The feds
even placed a bug in the nose of the moose.
If Doug stopped somewhere, decided not to
take the mount straight to his bar or home,
we had to be able to retrieve it.

It was evidence.

By early morning, we had men and unmarked vehicles on the ground from Rutland County to Granville, New York.

We had a relay set up. About six vehicles were scheduled to follow Doug from Shrewsbury to Rutland and west to Granville, switching on and off. The drivers would share information on where Doug was headed, how fast he was driving and if he stopped somewhere.

Yes, we could have planned to arrest Doug at Vinny's home. But we figured his ultimate plan was to take the mount to his bar in Granville, N.Y. and show it off.

The more state borders Doug crossed with his stolen prize, the deeper the hole he dug for himself in the eyes of the law.

We knew he had killed the moose in Maine, driven through New Hampshire and into Vermont. We wanted him to pick it up, make it clear the mount was his, and then drive into New York State.

But once again, Doug threw us a huge curve. Instead of 10 a.m., he showed up a little before 8 a.m. and almost blew the whole operation.

The wire on Vinny to record the conversation
with Doug?  It hadn't been attached yet.

Our timid taxidermist was still in his pajamas.
The agent assigned to get the room and Vinny
ready for Doug's arrival, leaped into a closet
and pulled the door shut to hide.

The airplane?  The pilot hadn't even arrived
at the airport yet.  The preflight check hadn't
been done.

Worse, Rutland was socked in with fog.
There would be no air surveillance.

But there was a tiny bit of good news.

When Vinny answered Doug's knock at the
back door, he began to apologize profusely for
not being ready for him, stood there in his
PJ's, stammered, trembled and smiled.

Doug didn't know Vinny well.  So whether
he thought Vinny was just stumbling about
because he was embarrassed at not being
ready for his customer or whether the glory of
the moose head on the table clouded Doug's
remarkable radar this one time—or maybe a
mix of both—we will never know.

Doug stepped inside, looked the moose head
over, nodded, laid an unmarked envelope on
the table with cash in it, picked up the mount
and turned to leave.

Vinny shuffled to the door and held it open
while Doug trotted nimbly out to his truck,
mostly hidden behind the long head and huge
expanse of antlers.

Doug looked both ways and quickly laid the
head in the back of his truck. He covered
the mount up with a used blue tarp, then put
some loose boards over the edges and part of
a hay bale on top, to make it look like he was
hauling junk.

He moved fast, no nonsense. Then he jumped
into his truck and headed west, towards
Route 4 in Fair Haven, Vermont.

Tailing him, taking turns with our vehicles, he
was followed.

Changing out vehicles and drivers, radioing
ahead, we all crossed our fingers. And with
every mile Doug drove west, those of us at
the end of the line who were waiting for him,
hidden, felt the tension rise.

When word arrived Doug had turned south off Route 4, and was headed through the center of Fair Haven, we got into our final positions and waited.

Less than two minutes later, Doug crossed from Vermont into New York. Six vehicles—carrying state and federal agents—came out of nowhere and boxed Doug in. With the shuttered Hampton Manor looking on, agents drew their weapons and pointed them straight at Doug.

He kept his hands firmly on the steering wheel but his smug smile turned to ashes. We had him at last.

Doug's arrest made headlines nationwide. Many people were outraged at the crime.

For his cooperation in helping federal prosecutors get Doug, Vinny was not charged. Maybe someone at the federal level figured he'd suffered enough. Maybe someone there realized federal criminal charges might literally kill the man.

I heard later Vinny decided taxidermy wasn't for him. He closed the door on that business venture.

As for Doug, he appeared before a federal judge in Vermont, facing $20,000 in fines as well as a prison sentence.

The prosecutor's office told the press Doug had been in their sights for some time. They were considering charging him with more crimes.

After several months of behind the scenes legal wrangling, Doug pled guilty. He paid a $10,000 fine.

Whether we ended Doug's poaching entirely, it's hard to say. But the case did change the way a lot of local people thought of him.

Doug was a guy who loved to talk about his hunting prowess. All those trophies he had hung on the wall of his bar? Doug had a story to tell about every one of them.

But now, people wondered if his stories were true. Had Doug really tracked that 10 point buck over two mountains in a blizzard? Did he really spend the night in a snow cave, then hike another three miles through a swamp before cornering the handsome 8 pointer?

Or was it more likely he climbed into his truck after locking up his bar around 3 a.m., cruised back roads, blinded the animals with a spotlight and pulled the trigger? Or maybe he paid others to do his dirty work?

Oh, Doug still had some friends and followers. But a lot of local people just didn't believe him anymore.

A few years later, as part of Granville's downtown renewal, Doug's Den and other bars along Water Street were demolished.

Looking at the area today, few would believe the sunny green lane was once a crowded alley teeming with characters worthy of a Charles Dickens' novel.

But those of us who spent countless cold nights chasing Doug and other poachers throughout the Mettawee Valley, we'll never forget.

*I saw the moose's nostrils flared wide with red
and pink. I heard the sucking sound of heavy
feet pulling out of the wet trail. The moose
was parting three and four inch saplings like
paper ribbons. He was only a few feet away.*

# MAD MOOSE

CONTRIBUTED BY KEN DENTON

When crickets croon and a gentle breeze stirs the poplar leaves in late September, I recall this moonless night and a chill runs up my spine.

Moose had made their way west across the Connecticut River from the Granite State. Their numbers were increasing in the Northeast Kingdom of Vermont, where I worked. We were a few years away from establishing a limited moose hunt and every moose was cherished like a cattle baron's prize breeding stock. Wardens, private land owners—all kinds of people—did our best to keep them out of harm's way.

A lot of people look upon moose as odd, ponderous swamp suckers. The Bullwinkle cartoon many of us grew up watching on TV portrays them as sweet, lovable and a little dimwitted.

And from a distance, moose are placid. But they are volatile and unpredictable if they feel threatened. It might be best to think of them as 1,000 pounds of pure panic.

Get too close for a moose to feel safe and it could just run off or it may charge and run right over you. Every moose has its own idea of how close is too close and it changes constantly.

A moose fights by slashing and pounding with their front hooves and using their rock hard head as a battering ram. Alaskan wildlife officials say moose, not bears, cause the most injuries to people.

In the Spring, moose cows with young calves are particularly dangerous. In the Fall, it is more likely the bulls—with mating on their mind—who will charge you. Only bulls grow antlers—which can grow up to five feet wide. Hard as bone and with sharp points, they are used to clash with other males during mating season, to prove superiority. If you were unfortunate enough to be attacked by a bull moose, add being gored by antlers to your list of injuries.

Moose pose a threat even to those who never set foot in the woods. Anyone riding in a vehicle in moose country is at risk. Just like their smaller cousins, whitetail deer, moose don't look both ways before they step into traffic. And because moose are three and four times the size of deer, drivers are a lot more likely to be injured if they strike one.

Hooved animals are at a disadvantage on highways. Their feet cannot get traction. As fast as deer and moose are on land, their hooves slip and slide on asphalt, slowing them, causing them to fall.

Moose stand so tall above most vehicles their eyes do not reflect headlights. Most drivers who strike a moose say they never even saw the animal.

When a moose is hit by a vehicle, their legs go out from under them and their body comes crashing down, often on the roof. Drivers and passengers have little protection. Slowing down in moose country at all times of the year and avoiding driving at night on roads where moose are known to cross is about your only real protection.

Being struck by a vehicle almost always means the moose has to be euthanized. Their long legs just can't take a hit from the side.

Moving through the woods takes balance. Moose can suffer for days, even weeks with a broken leg. Sometimes both hind legs are broken and the animal drags its body with its forelegs for days.

So, while a warden tracking an injured animal and shooting it may sound harsh, it is really the most humane thing to do.

That's why when I got a call late one moonless night, about a pickup truck having hit a moose on the Granby Road, I rushed over.

I found the driver by the side of the road, waiting for me. He told me he had worked a late shift and was headed home when a bull moose stepped right in front of him. He saw antlers, a big blotch of dark brown, but didn't even have time to brake. He told me he spun the steering wheel, trying to avoid the animal, but still clipped it in the back. The bull fell onto the road, scrambled up and then took off into the night.

I shined my flashlight over the front of his pick up. The bumper was bent back and the right fender wrinkled badly. The fellow told me he wasn't hurt and he believed he could drive his truck home. But he wasn't so sure about the moose. He thought it might have a broken leg.

We walked the road shoulder together, so he could point out where he had hit the moose and which way it had headed. I found cloven hoof prints bigger than my hand and knew only a bull moose could have made them. They matched the story the driver told me.

I thanked the fellow and said I would follow the moose. If it had to be put down, I wouldn't let it suffer and the meat would go to feed the hungry. He nodded, thanked me, climbed back into his pickup and drove away.

I walked back to my truck and shoved three slugs into my shotgun's magazine, slid the fore end back and forward to push a shell into the firing chamber, and made certain the safety was on.

With my flashlight in my left hand and my shotgun in my right, I stepped into the grass to hunt for the bull.

I lifted my flashlight to look closer at where
the moose was headed.

There was tall grass for 100 feet or so and
then the land rose slightly and turned into
thousands of small trees and leafy shrubs.
Behind the young growth was a stand of mixed
hardwoods.

I followed the fresh moose prints through the
grass and within a few of its paces saw the
hoof prints left by the big bull were off. The
moose was not putting its full weight on both
back legs.

One leg was dragging slightly. And in another
few steps, it was clear the bull's front hooves
were digging deeper into the soft ground,
like the front was working extra hard to
compensate for that injured back leg.

I paused and listened for the sound of
movement around me in the brush. There was
a good chance the moose had not run far, had
collapsed somewhere. If so, it would be easy to
dispatch it.

I raised my light and looked around. If it was
lying down, I should at least see antlers. But

no antlers or eyes reflected in my light. And the only sound was of crickets and night insects singing, and a gentle whoosh of a light night breeze washing over the tall grass.

I lowered my light and kept on the animal's tracks, which took me to the edge of the young forest. Even though Autumn was upon us, this mixed stand held most of its leaves.

The tangle of trees and tall reeds and bushes prompted me to pause a second. "It is going to be really tough to see in there. I'm going to have to be extra careful," I said to myself.

I was used to going into the woods at night to find a deer or a bear struck by a vehicle. But I wanted to be smart and not just stumble onto an injured bull moose.

I had worked to redirect cow moose who had wandered into residential areas before and had watched them panic and bolt. Both came so close to me I could have reached out and touched them. With a bull, I might not be as lucky.

Flashlights are great when pointed down at the earth, looking for tracks. But pointed straight ahead in dense growth it is hard to distinguish between objects. I knew I would not be able to see more than a few feet ahead of me.

I parted two stems and stepped inside.

I saw a lot of moose had been using this area. There were trails punched deep with cloven tracks and snapped stems and branches beneath the canopy of birches and alders.

Some of the trees stood 10 feet tall. Others were right at eye level. Where the sunlight had managed to shine beneath the tree canopy, six and eight feet tall bushes flourished.

With their long legs and powerful shoulders, moose could step over the broken and downed trees like so many leaves of grass. But for me, it would be tough going. There were no trees big enough to climb if I got in trouble.

I knew I had to rely on my hearing as much as my vision. Within 20 paces, I felt like I was standing in the middle of a thousand wind chimes made of seashells. My flashlight reflected an ever changing muddle of silver

and gray and black. The leaves of the young
poplar trees shook and shimmied in my light
beam, playing tricks with my eyes.

I stayed on the moose's trail, took a few steps,
stopped and listened.

I found myself frequently twisting my
shoulders to part the aspen whips, birches and
reeds—then leaning forward—to peer into the
dark. All the time I kept my left hand on my
light shining straight in front of me and my
shotgun in my right hand, my trigger finger
just outside the guard.

Just the sound of my clothing sliding past
branches could signal the moose I was coming.
Scientists believe bull moose can hear up to
two miles and antlers actually enhance their
hearing.

I took another five steps and found the trees
opening up a bit. In their place were reeds and
wetland brush six and eight feet tall, blocking
much of my view, towering over me.

It seemed to me the moose was headed to
the hardwoods above. I knew if he got that
far, it would be easier for me to see him but

he might also make a run for it. And even
with a broken leg, he could traverse a lot
more ground than a man on two good legs. I
wanted to catch up to him before he got much
farther.

I stopped again to listen and heard only the
leaves fluttering.

I took a breath and lifted a foot to step over a
downed sapling. Up in front of me, maybe 80
feet ahead, I heard a branch snap and leaves
brushed aside.

I figured it was my moose, just ahead. It
was time for me to move faster, maybe circle
around him a bit, cut him off, find him and
finish him.

I gritted my teeth and picked up my pace
along the trail. My flashlight and shotgun
remained pointed directly in front of me.

I had forged ahead maybe 15 feet, when who
was chasing who changed big time.

I heard the woods erupt in front of me, maybe
50 feet away. Tree branches snapped and
cracked and tree trunks knocked into one

another like a child running down a sidewalk holding a stick against a picket fence.

Something very big was headed for me.

I backed up several paces. I needed to see what was coming, to identify my target before I pulled the trigger. I knew if I stepped back fast, I could trip and fall. There were no trees big enough to hide behind.

I held my light straight in front of me in my left hand. In my right hand I kept my shotgun pointed straight ahead and pushed the safety off.

I heard hooves pounding the mud. Treetops rocked and lashed one another in front of me and I saw a huge solid shadow, coming closer.

Leaves flew up and sifted down into my flashlight beam.

I held my ground.

I finally saw a wide brown muzzle aiming for my head. I pulled the trigger.

Nothing happened. My shotgun didn't fire. The animal was getting closer. Powerful hairy

shoulders towered above my head and filled
my view.

The gentle rustle of leaves was replaced with
a whoosh, like a giant was loose in the woods
and using entire trees to swat mosquitos.

All around me trees were being knocked,
scraped, raked, slammed and splintered.
It was like I was standing in the path of a
bulldozer

I extended my fingers over the flashlight
handle, grabbed the pump and shuttled the
slide down and forward again as fast as I
could.  I pulled the trigger on my shotgun a
second time.

Nothing.  Once again, my shotgun didn't fire.
The shell kicked out and jumped into the weeds.

I realized I must have short stroked the
shotgun again—the slug had not entered the
firing chamber.

I had to try again.  It was my last chance.
This was no skeet shooting competition, no
partridge hunt.  My life was at stake with the
next shell.  I had to get it right this time.

I saw the moose's nostrils flared wide with red and pink. I heard the sucking sound of heavy feet pulling out of the wet trail. The moose was parting three and four inch saplings like paper ribbons and only a few feet away.

I was about to be trampled.

I reached again for the fore end and pulled it back and threw it forward a third time. The moose filled my light—massive brown shoulders, a muzzle bigger than my head and a four foot spread of sharp antlers.

Last chance. I pulled the trigger.

The gun fired. The gunpowder blast colored the night for a micro second. The bull's antlers shimmered silver. The brown head was a red orange and the deep brown body was highlighted in purple—the stuff of nightmares.

The moose stumbled, its front knees collapsed and the animal pitched forward. The wide antlers raked the trees around me and I jumped back to avoid getting hit. The animal toppled and its chin landed six inches from my boots. I could reach out and touch the antlers.

I stepped back slowly, still keeping an eye on the moose. The trees that weren't broken, snapped back to their upright position and rocked, sending another shower of leaves falling on my head and shoulders.

I took a few deep breaths, then found the shell that had kicked out of my shotgun. I wiped it off and quickly slid it back into the Remington's magazine—just in case this bull had another big friend nearby.

When my heartbeat slowed, I looked the animal over more closely. It was a mature bull, maybe five years old and around 850 pounds. I stepped over and around the tangle of broken saplings and shined my light over the animal. A hind leg was broken.

From the time I heard the bull, until my shotgun finally fired, was probably only four seconds. But it was the longest four seconds of my life.

Over the years, I have tried to figure out why the moose came back down the trail, at me. Did it hear me behind it? Did it see my flashlight beam—white light in the night —and equate that with the truck headlights?

Was there a bigger, older bull somewhere
farther up the trail and it decided to turn
around?

Why it came after me, I'll never know.
I sure didn't expect it. I guess that's what
everybody who gets run over by a moose
says—if they live.

As I drove home that night, I thought back to
stories of big game hunting in Africa I read
when I was a boy. Stories of water buffalo
jumping up from the brush and charging.

It was thrilling reading for a youngster in
the Northeast Kingdom, barely old enough to
hunt squirrels.

I realized I didn't have to travel to Africa for
that kind of adventure anymore.

Moose had returned to Vermont.

When the door opened, she just stood
there staring at us, a few feet away.
In her jaws was a deflated black
plastic garbage bag.

# Love My Gun

CONTRIBUTED BY KEN DENTON AND WALT ACKERMANN

Here's a philosophical question for you: Can you love your deer rifle too much? I'll let you decide.

Nick had been caught poaching deer before. To make the case against him air tight, I asked the state lab to run the ballistics on Nick's rifle and the lead we found in the dead deer he left behind.

The lab report came back a match. Nick was convicted of the crime and his rifle—a Mauser, made in Germany and famous for their smooth bolt action—was confiscated.

Nick's rifle was now in the state's gun cabinet, away from Nick's itchy trigger finger.

Thing was, Nick really liked his Mauser. He wanted the rifle back. So he asked for the deer rifle to be returned to him.

It's a little unusual for a fellow convicted of poaching to bother with this. You have to write letters and wait. It's critical for the person to first complete whatever the court gave them as punishment and to stay out of trouble with the law.

It takes time for the wheels of justice to turn. Sometimes a lot of time.

Most people just go and purchase another rifle if they want to go deer hunting.

There are Mausers worth a lot of money, but Nick's wasn't one of them. Still, for whatever reason, Nick decided his rifle was worth the trouble of petitioning the court to get it back. And eventually, he did.

When I heard the rifle was back with Nick, I filed it mentally under, "Hunh" and just hoped he would use it to hunt legally.

And for a long time, I didn't have any problems that would lead me to think Nick might be involved.

Three years later, my cruiser radio came to life with a call about a shot in the night near Martins Pond in Peacham.

I was 35 minutes away. By the time I arrived, there was no sign of a vehicle or a shooter.

Still, I got out of the cruiser and walked the roadsides with my flashlight shining bright, searching for clues. I found where a poacher had driven off the road, shot a doe, removed the hindquarters and back straps and driven off.

The head, neck, ribs, legs—everything but what hunters consider the best cuts—were still lying there. The poacher was in a hurry or just didn't care about wasting a lot of meat.

I was too late to catch the poacher red handed. But that didn't mean the fellow might not have left me some clues. Most deer jackers are in too much of a hurry to take the time to cover up their crime.

I looked the deer over carefully and found where the fatal shot had entered the doe's body. I reached under the deer and felt around for an exit wound. A bullet will generally be felt as a lump beneath the skin on the other side of the animal.

Sure enough, I found it. I turned the deer carcass over, reached into my pants pocket, removed the razor sharp folding knife I carried and slid the blade open.

With my flashlight in one hand, I carefully slit
the hide and dug out the shot with my other hand.
Then I wiped the blade on the grass, closed up
my knife and slid it back into my pocket.

Now it was time to look more closely at the
bullet. Thanks in part to the copper jacket
used in modern ballistics, the projectile was all
in one piece. It hadn't shattered inside the deer.
That was good news.

I pulled an evidence bag from my jacket,
dropped the bullet inside it and stood up.

Then I rubbed my hands on the grass around
me to clean them a bit and walked back to my
cruiser.

Once inside, I jotted down my notes, then
held the bag up to the dome light and started
speculating on potential suspects. They were
all guys I had caught poaching deer at one time
or another and it was a pretty lengthy list.

But staring at that chunk of copper topped lead,
I got a funny feeling and a name jumped into
my head.

Nick. He certainly wasn't the only fellow who
might have done this. There were many I'd busted

before and others I probably never would. But for whatever reason, that bullet screamed, "Nick."

But you can't get a search warrant based on a funny feeling.

I drove the bullet over to the lab the next morning. Two weeks later, I got a phone call informing me it matched one from a rifle tested four years earlier, in another deer poaching case.

That rifle was a Mauser owned by....
You guessed it. I couldn't help but smile.
I felt pretty good about my intuition.

Since Nick had wanted the rifle back so badly he'd waited almost two years to get it, there was little question in my mind he still owned it. It didn't make sense he would let it go. But would he suspect we would be looking for the rifle? Would he have hidden it somewhere?

The combination of the dead doe and the lab report stating the weapon used was Nick's, gave me what I needed to get a search warrant of his house.

The job now was to surprise him at home, find the rifle in his possession, maybe find some of the venison, then charge him.

But Nick was not an easy guy to deal with. He
could be calm as a mountain pond one minute,
then explode like a lightning bolt the next.

And while you never quite knew what it was
that would trigger his rage, it was guaranteed
law enforcement officers stopping to have a chat
with him would do it.

His eyes would flash daggers, the cords in his
neck would tighten like piano wire and Nick
would wave his arms and shout, saying he was
going to get a gun and kill everyone of us.

He wasn't a huge guy. A little under 6 feet tall.
But he worked as a farm hand and had since
he was a youngster. Nick was a "rugged lad," as
old timers would say. Broad shoulders, legs and
back. He had the physique to be a real threat.

It's one situation to deal with a volatile fellow
like Nick out in the open. But to knock on their
door and enter their home, saying you are there
to search through all their stuff?

That's the sort of move that can get law officers
killed.

You step inside the door and reach for your
warrant and they reach behind the kitchen

door for their shotgun.  Or you are standing in the kitchen chatting amiably and they find a foot long kitchen knife and come at you with it.

You just never know.

Could be a suspect had a fight with his boss earlier in the week, bills he can't pay, or the wife and he have been arguing about who knows what.  A visit from a fellow with a badge can be the last straw.

I wanted to make certain Nick behaved while we searched his house for the rifle.  I didn't want anyone hurt.

So, I called Deputy Warden Walt Ackermann and a couple of state police officers and they agreed to come along with me as back up. We converged on Nick's house on a cold gray October afternoon.  Farm chores were over and his truck was parked in the driveway.

Search warrant in my hand, I led the way to the front door and knocked.  I expected Nick to yank the door open and go berzerk.

But instead, he opened the door slightly, and listened.  He wasn't exactly polite, but he didn't immediately call us every name in the book and accuse us of harassing him.

I told Nick there had been a doe shot at Martins Pond a few weeks ago and the bullet found matched his rifle. I had obtained a warrant allowing us to search for the Mauser and any other evidence that might be related to the crime.

He looked down at the floor, nodded and after a few seconds said softly, "Uh. Okay. Come in."

The door took us right inside the kitchen. I saw Nick look behind him, over his shoulder to a dark corner where a big German Shepherd was tied. The dog was standing silently, watching us.

"Uh. Wait a minute! Just wait a minute. Let me put my dog in the bedroom before you come any closer. I don't want her to bite any of you guys. She can be really vicious," he said with alarm in his voice.

I looked closer at the dog. She wasn't growling. She was just standing there watching us. She yawned, opened her mouth in a big doggie smile. I saw she had plenty of long pearly whites to do damage. But she wasn't acting aggressive, just curious.

Still, better safe than sorry.

"Sure. Go ahead," I said to Nick. "Take her in the other room." Nick turned, bent low, released the snap from her lead, got several fingers beneath her leather collar and led his dog around the corner. He was talking in soothing tones all the while.

Walt walked over and watched Nick go down the hall, to make certain there was no funny business.

In a few seconds, I heard the door hinges creak to a close, the latch clicked shut and Nick returned to the kitchen.

He cleared his throat, breathed a sigh of relief and stood three feet in front of the state police and me, quiet as a good schoolboy.

I was waiting for the yelling to start. I began to think maybe Nick had gotten some help for his anger issues.

"Nick, I'm going to ask you a few questions while Walt searches your house, okay?"

Silently, I counted to three. I just knew this guy was going to blow like some volcano.

Nick took a deep breath and exhaled slowly.
Then he looked me in the eye and a look of
resignation crossed his face. He shrugged his
shoulders and said, "Okay. You got me.
I'll get it for you."

Nick took three steps over to his refrigerator,
opened it and pulled out two bags of fresh
venison and put them on the kitchen table.
Then he jerked open the freezer compartment,
placed a carton of ice cream and a couple of
frozen pizzas on the kitchen table, and reached
way in back to grab some frozen venison. He
put those packages on the kitchen table too.
He picked up the ice cream and pizza cartons,
tossed them back inside the freezer, shut the
appliance doors, turned and looked at us.

I didn't say a word. None of us did. I was
in shock. I had never seen this guy be so
cooperative.

Nick looked over at Walt, turned his head
towards the living room and said, "My deer rifle
is in the corner over there, behind the curtain.
Go ahead. Take it."

Walt and one of the troopers strolled into the
room to find it. I stayed with Nick and the
second trooper stuck with me.

"Thank you," I told Nick. "We appreciate your cooperation here."

Walt returned with the Mauser in his hands. He had made certain the gun was not loaded and opened the action.

I had everything I needed to make a case. The only thing left was for Nick to give us a signed confession. But, his behavior was so out of character for this powder keg of a man, we couldn't help but wonder if something else was going on.

I looked over at Walt and nodded slightly. "We're going to search your house for more evidence," I said. I saw Nick's body stiffen when the words came out of my mouth.

Walt returned to the living room, looked in cabinets, under couch cushions, gave the room a good once over and put everything back where he found it.

I continued to observe Nick in the kitchen. He fidgeted a bit and then began confessing to more poaching. "Do you want the turkey too?" he asked me. "If you step outside, I'll get it for you," he sighed. "There's a chest freezer out in the shed."

When I didn't immediately head outdoors, he added, "Uh, there's some partridge out there too."

This was too good to be true. Nick was not only giving us everything we needed for the dead doe case, he was confessing to more poaching.

My mind was shouting, "There's something else going on here. What is this guy hiding? What does he not want us to find?"

Walt came back from the living room and stood quietly. I saw one of his eyebrows shoot up when Nick suggested we all step outside.

Walt and I had been at this game a long time. We knew if the suspect wanted to show you something outside, it was because there was something inside he didn't want you to see. The state troopers didn't say a word. But I knew they were thinking the same thing.

The four of us looked at Nick in stunned silence. That's when we heard scratching, clawing and whining at the other end of the house. It was the dog. She was making very clear she did not like being locked away from the action.

Nick pretended like he didn't hear her. Strange.

"I want to search that room," I said to Nick. "The one with your dog in it."

"Oh, I wouldn't go in there," Nick said shaking his head from side to side, his eyes widening and the color draining from his face. "She'll attack. I don't want any of you guys bit. And I don't want you shooting my dog either."

"Well, then you need to get control of your dog," I told Nick. "But we're going inside that room." Nick protested even more. "No. Really. Don't do it. She'll bite you."

I wasn't eager to get bit. But the warrant gave us the right to search the premises—all of it— and we needed to do it. Something very fishy was going on.

"Let's go, Nick," I told him. "You walk in front of me and get ahold of your dog when I open the door. That way, no one will be hurt."

The dog heard us coming. She clawed more feverishly at the door, yipped and cried. It was a little unnerving. I couldn't tell if the dog wanted to tear into us or she just didn't like being left alone.

I was within three feet of the closed door, right behind Nick, when I heard something being shaken violently. It was sort of a rustling sound, like dry leaves in a bag, but at the speed of a paint shaker.

I stopped and cocked my head towards the door, leaned in and listened. It was like the mutt was tearing the room apart. I knew some dogs grab whatever is close and rip and chew out of frustration when they can't sink their teeth into what they really want—the postman or maybe a game warden.

Is this big Shepherd so vicious she's destroying the furniture? Is my leg next?

Nick used his body to block the door opening. It was like he was my guardian angel.

He turned and said, "You hear that?" like he had a furry shark on the other side of the door. He pleaded with me one more time to give up on opening that door.

"Really, you shouldn't go in there," he said. His eyes were the size of silver dollars.

"I'll turn the handle. You get your dog," I told him. "On the count of three." Walt bent down behind me like a shortstop, ready to make a

grab for the dog if she came racing out and
Nick missed her collar.

I turned the door handle, opened it wide and
leaped back like a matador with a bull coming
at him.

The dog was smart. She must have been
slapped in the nose by a door before.

When the door opened, she just stood there
staring at us, a few feet away. In her jaws was
a deflated black plastic garbage bag. It was
punched full of doggie teeth marks and had
ragged holes with pencil like sticks poking out.

The floor beneath her big paws was strewn
with green leaves and twigs. She was so mad
at being ostracized from the action, she had
grabbed the sack and shook it to pieces.

With the door wide open, the pooch dropped the
bag and pranced out, her tail wagging and a
big white doggie grin on her face as she trotted
between Nick and me.

Nick's shoulders slumped. He didn't even reach
for her. Walt and I were so stunned at the scene
before us, we just let her go too.

I stood dumbstruck at an impressive marijuana garden. It was like standing on the edge of the Amazon jungle. There was cannabis in every stage of life—10 inchers to 10 footers. Fifty pound bags of peat moss, fertilizer, potting soil and watering cans were stacked in one corner.

Nick had removed the ceiling tiles in sections of the room and tied rope to the rafters to keep his biggest plants upright. There were power tools and chainsaws and even jewelry piled in another corner. That made me wonder if maybe Nick might be burglarizing homes too. Or maybe people traded him their loot for dope?

After a few seconds of stunned silence, I turned to the troopers down the hall and said, "Gentlemen, you need to come take a look at this."

I stepped back—still with an eye on Nick—and the troopers passed me in the hall to survey the botanical garden. Within two minutes, a trooper had gone to his car to request a second search warrant of Nick's home. This one would cover illegal drugs, drug paraphernalia and stolen goods.

Walt and I, Nick and the dog headed back into the kitchen. Nick and I sat down at the table and waited.

There was some awkward silence on Nick's part, but it wasn't too bad. I figured he was using that time to come up with a story he could tell the state police of how all that dope got into his house. Or maybe he was thinking of a good attorney to call to defend him.

Nick left in handcuffs later that night. He was charged with a long list of crimes, including poaching.

His Mauser went back into the hands of the state. And this time, Nick didn't get it back. He ended up with a felony conviction and a jail sentence. He can never own a gun again.

So, what do you think?

Can you love your gun too much?

*The husband walked slowly towards the headboard, leaned down and grabbed a handful of white chenille bedspread, blanket and top sheet.*

# COLD COMFORT

CONTRIBUTED BY KEN DENTON AND WALT ACKERMANN

I stopped by the office and was handed a note by the Dispatcher.

It looked like it had been shuffled off to the side, then sifted slowly down into a paper pile like a pebble thrown into a wet field. The corners were bent, the paper crinkled.

I looked at the date and time in the upper right corner. Sure enough, it was written three days earlier. I shook my head.

The memo said a man had phoned and refused to give his name. He said he thought a neighbor in his apartment building had shot and killed a deer.

The season had closed. If the report was true, this was poaching.

There was a street address and the number of an apartment—that was it. There was no return phone number.

I scowled a little and shook my head.

The voice of experience told me the chance of finding any evidence of a deer having been taken illegally three days ago were about nil. Any drops of blood would have been cleaned up. The unwanted remains—head, hooves and hide—would be gone. The rifle would have been cleaned and put away.

Venison in the home? Maybe. But even then, a lot of people make certain to store it somewhere else.

But they didn't pay me to speculate. My job was to look into things.

I gave Deputy Walt Ackermann a call and asked if he had time to ride with me to chat with whoever answered the door and check things out. Two sets of eyes would be better than one. While I was asking questions, my deputy could be looking around a room for clues.

I figured supper was the best time to pay a visit.

If we were really lucky, the guy would be frying up some fresh venison and have to come up with a quick story to explain how he acquired it.

It was about 6 p.m. when we got to the apartment house, which from the electric meters hanging on the side of the building, told me it held four units.

We didn't bother to knock on doors to find the neighbor who called in the complaint. We had all we were going to get from him and didn't want to give the suspect any clue as to who might have tipped us off.

There was no need to create problems between neighbors. Just how I had been tipped off would remain my little secret.

Walt and I parked the truck, got out and walked upstairs to the suspect's door.

As I climbed the stairs, I tried to quiet my doubts. Not many people have a freezer in

their apartment to keep 50 or more pounds
of venison.

Then there is the challenge of getting rid of
the hide, the head, legs, hooves and more.
Where would a fellow living in a second story
apartment get rid of all that?

But nothing ventured, nothing gained, right?

I knocked on the door with authority, me in
my uniform and Walt in his. In less than a
minute a fellow around 30 years old with sandy
hair turned the handle and opened the door a
crack.

When he saw the badge and brass, his eyes
went wide and his head snapped back. It was
like he was a new Army recruit and his drill
sergeant had entered the barracks, shouting.

If the fellow had just been blasted with a charge
of "frozen human" he could not have been
stiffer. His reaction to our showing up at his
door made me think maybe the tip was true.

"We'd like to talk to you," I said to him.
I could hear a TV inside and the anchors at
WCAX reporting the day's news.

"Uh, geez," he replied, his eyes darting from one side of the hallway to the other, like he was looking for an escape. "Uh, my wife isn't decent."

As soon as he said that, he stopped himself, realizing that's a strange thing to say.

I kept my eyes on him for more signs of internal squirming.

He closed his eyes and shook his head like he was shaking water from his hair after a shower. Then he opened his eyes, took a deep breath and started over.

"I mean, she's not dressed for visitors," he said emphasizing every word and smiling like he was apologizing for the confusion.

The door was open maybe a third of the way and it was clear he didn't intend to invite us in.

Not yet anyway.

"Well, we'd like to come in," I said.

He peered off over his left shoulder. He was looking at something. The wife, maybe?

Then he turned back towards me and said, "Uh, just a minute, please. I'll be right back."

He shut the front door, leaving us to stand in the hallway.

I looked over at Walt. Walt looked at me and shrugged.

I was thinking, "This fellow is acting a little too nervous, like he's got something going on inside his place. Something he wants to hide."

Then again, it could be his wife liked to slip out of her office clothes after work and get comfortable in a torn shirt and sweatpants. She might be unprepared to greet the officers at her door.

I leaned in closer to the door and cocked my head to listen. If he was discussing deer or venison with his wife, I wanted to hear it.

There was some whispering all right, but I couldn't make out the conversation with the TV on.

We stood in the hallway waiting. Time dragged on. I looked at my watch. The husband had left us nearly five minutes earlier. Walt and I were a little perturbed.

Walt glowered at the door handle. After 20 seconds, he gave up and turned away. He pursed his lips and started tapping his toe on the worn hallway carpet to pass the time.

Without a search warrant, we couldn't go inside the home if the couple did not want us in there.

I wondered if the guy was thinking about just sending us away. If he did that, we were done. All I had was an old tip from a neighbor who refused to even give their name. The chances of a judge giving me a search warrant based on an anonymous tip were nil.

Just when I was thinking we could be out of luck, I heard footsteps coming towards us.

He threw the door open wide and smiled at Walt and me like a used car salesman greeting his first customer of the day onto the lot.

"Sorry to keep you waiting," he said with a forced smile and slightly damp brow. "My wife

doesn't feel well.  She's decided to just go to bed.
Come on in."

I nodded and stepped inside.  Walt followed.
I relied on deputies like Walt to scout a room
for clues while I chatted with people to get
their story.

The couple had a neatly kept home and it looked
like they were getting ready for dinner.  There
was a box on the counter with the lid opened.
A stick of butter and a knife lay atop a plate.

To my left was the living area with a floral
couch, a faux leather recliner and a few other
stuffed chairs.  Neatly stacked magazines sat
on an end table.  Off to the right was a small
kitchen and in it, the couple's refrigerator.

The husband turned towards the living area,
but I stopped him short.  It was the kitchen we
were interested in.

The guy turned to face me, a bit shocked I didn't
just follow him to the sitting area.  He looked
like a youngster who had been leading his pony
from a dusty pen to the barn, when the pony
stopped dead in its tracks, put its head down
and grabbed for grass.

"We got a tip you took a deer out of season,"
I said to him.

As soon as the word "deer" crossed my lips, his
hands came together and he began spinning
his wedding band with a couple of nervous
fingers.

"No.  No.  I don't know anything about that,"
he stammered.  "There's no deer here."

While I had the fellow's eyes trained on me, I
asked, "Mind if we look in your refrigerator?"
Walt took two big steps and stood inches from
the appliance.

He was like a bird dog poised to flush grouse
from a thicket.  Give the word and Walt would
dive in, methodically searching for evidence.

The fellow shrugged his shoulders and said
confidently, "Sure."

Walt pulled the latch on the white door, bent
low and poked around behind the milk, butter
and eggs.  He gave each shelf a good once over
—pulling drawers and moving bottles around
inside.  Then he stood up, looked at me and
shook his head.

Now, it was the freezer's turn. Walt opened the smaller door and poked his nose inside. I stood beside the suspect, watching his reaction while peering into the freezer from 10 feet away.

I couldn't help but notice a big hole next to what appeared to be a bag of frozen vegetables and a couple of trays of ice cubes.

That hole was suspicious. Most people toss bags in the freezer when they rush home from the grocery store. It all settles into a sloppy frozen pile. When they want a meal, they open the door and paw through the mess quickly.

Even the folks who organize and label every item don't leave a hole on one side. They'd fill it with some item and pile new purchases on top. It looked like maybe someone had reached inside that freezer a few minutes ago.

But the oven light wasn't on. There was nothing cooking on top of the stove. And it didn't smell like anything had been cooking either.

Walt poked around the freezer, going so far as to pull items out and balance them on his left arm like a waitress carrying a stack of

trays.  He had a carton of ice cream sitting
on his shoulder, then a couple bags of mixed
vegetables and a frozen pizza resting on top of
his arm.  He used his free hand to push items
around inside the freezer.

Just when I thought this search was going to
be a bust, I saw Walt stop cold—forgive the
pun—and stare.

He squinted and dipped his head to the right,
almost sticking it inside the compartment.  He
widened his stance on the kitchen floor—to get
lower—dipped his right shoulder and let the
ice cream carton on his left shoulder slide and
smack him in the side of the head.

In a kind of twisty limbo dancer move, his right
hand and forearm disappeared deep into the
ice chest.

I looked at Walt, admiring his ability to dig
into a freezer with bare hands and search
thoroughly despite the cold, then looked over at
the husband.  The fellow had an "Uh oh" look
on his face.

He looked like a guy who had planned a
weekend in the woods, hiked in, got his

sleeping bag set up and his campfire, then felt the call of Nature and reached for the toilet paper, only to realize he forgot to pack it.

Walt's hand came out of the freezer holding a package wrapped in white butcher paper. He had a tiny "gotcha" smile on his face as he handed it to me.

One by one, Walt peeled the frozen items off his left arm with his right hand and put them neatly back inside the couple's freezer. Then he shut the door and turned to face me.

I held the mystery packet in my right hand and lifted it up and down, estimating its weight and letting the owner take a good look at what Walt had found in his fridge. I figured it weighed close to five pounds. The white wrap had crisply folded edges—that implied it was new. It might have been way in the back, but the item hadn't been inside that freezer long.

Someone had written "Party Pack" on the outside with a black marker. That was odd too. Generally, frozen meat packages say roast, chops, stew meat—something specific.

"Mind if I open this?" I asked the fellow.

He looked down at the floor for a second,
sighed, raised his head and looked back up
at me like a gangly puppy that had just been
caught with his paws on the counter gnawing
on the Thanksgiving turkey.

"Okay," he said softly.

I peeled back the freezer tape on one end.
There in front of me were three fat brown deer
hairs, sitting atop dark red meat.

I lowered the packet, put it right in front of the
fellow, so he would see what I had just seen.

Then I turned to Walt said out loud what all
three of us knew.

"It's deer meat, venison." I passed the frozen
package back over to Walt and nodded.

Walt and I glowered at the guy, who seemed to
be getting smaller by the minute. His shoulders
slumped and his knees buckled a bit. He
looked like he would have liked to sink into the
floor and disappear.

"Where's the rest of it?" I asked him in a stern
voice.

The fellow turned to look at Walt—looking for some sympathy, maybe. What he found was another uniformed officer standing tall and glaring at him, wanting an honest answer.

There was a long pause as he mulled over his options. The only noise in the apartment was the WCAX news crew, now giving us the weather forecast.

Maybe the fellow felt some guilt. Maybe he had a long day at work and just wanted his supper and our standing there asking questions was keeping him from his dinner. Maybe he was thinking of his wife.

Finally, he inhaled deeply, sighed and spoke. "This way," he said, and pointed towards a hallway.

He led us out of the kitchen to a closed door, stopped and knocked softly. Walt and I were right on his heels.

"Honey? I'm bringing the wardens in," he said, raising his voice a little.

He paused a couple seconds, grimaced as he turned the knob and opened the door slowly.

The blinds were drawn and the room was quite dark.

I saw a human figure under the covers on a double bed, facing the wall. I assumed it was his wife. Her back was to us.

The husband walked slowly towards the headboard, leaned down and grabbed a handful of white chenille bedspread, blanket and top sheet. He walked to the footboard and peeled back the covers, as if he was about to change the sheets.

He had a look on his face like the covers were a bandage on a sticky knee and this move was gonna hurt.

Tucked tight to the backside of his wife— dressed in a flannel nightgown—were about two dozen packages of fresh and frozen venison. Each was neatly wrapped in white butcher paper, taped shut and labeled: stew meat, steak, roast.

The woman's shoulders quivered. She didn't say a word. She didn't even turn over to face us. She may have thought it best to just pretend she was asleep and let her husband squirm.

Walt bent down and picked up a small package near the woman's ankles. He opened it, took a look, nodded and looked back up at me. "Yup. Venison," he said with a sly smile.

"Why don't we go back into the kitchen and have a talk?" I said to the husband.

"Deputy Ackermann will gather up the evidence. I'm sure your wife will be happy to assist him."

I figured the wife would want to separate her backside from the frozen venison as fast as possible. The poor woman was likely longing for a steamy hot shower.

I followed the fellow back to the kitchen table, where he flopped into a chrome chair and told me what happened.

He said he saw a small buck strolling through a deserted St. Johnsbury parking lot three days earlier.

After hunting all season and coming up empty, he said he just couldn't resist taking the shot.

It was early in the morning.  He didn't think anyone was watching.

He shot it, ran and got it, tossed the buck into the back of his truck and brought it home. He used the basement in the apartment house to cut it up.

As I wrote him a citation, Walt left the apartment and returned a minute later with an empty cooler.

He walked down the hall and gathered up all the venison, to take with us.  He brought the cooler loaded with meat back into the kitchen, and waited for me.

I was handing the fellow his citation when the TV screen flashed to a familiar commercial.

It grabbed our attention.

It was an "Operation Game Thief" public service announcement, urging people to call a toll free number to report poachers.

Walt and I shot each other a knowing look. Sure seemed like someone had taken the advice.

I wished the fellow a good evening. He kept his head down, took the citation and nodded. Walt picked up the cooler and we proceeded out to the truck.

When we were settled inside the cab, Walt said, "Have you checked your watch?"

"Should I?" I asked him as I halted my right arm reach for the truck key ignition.

"Well, yes," he said with big emphasis on the second word. "I think we just set a record."

I turned on the truck engine and pulled out of the yard. If the couple was watching out a window, I wanted to be out of sight.

"How's that?" I asked him as we pulled out into traffic.

"We solved that case in 46 minutes by my watch," Walt said. "From the knock on their door to just now."

"Really?" I asked.

"Yes," Walt went on. "And that's with the fellow making us wait in the hall five minutes. That's fast. It has to be a record, don't you think?"

I smiled big. "By golly, you may be right, Walt," I said. "This may be the fastest we've ever wrapped up an investigation."

There was a pause while each of us silently rolled through the years in our minds.

Walt again broke the silence.

"You know, it's a really good thing we wrapped this case up quick," Walt declared.

"How's that?" I asked him.

"Well, that poor woman could have ended up with some serious freezer burn," Walt laughed.

*I was so close to the open*
*field, so close to the carcass!*
*If a bright light shined the area,*
*they would surely see me.*

# No Anglais

CONTRIBUTED BY KEN DENTON

The opening weekend of deer rifle season was behind me. It was the middle of the week and there was a welcome lull. This evening, I was using the quiet to get caught up on some paperwork. I was about an hour into the large pile on my desk when the phone rang.

The caller said he and his wife had heard a gunshot just down the road near his neighbor's boarded up dairy farm. He told me he had heard a noisy muffler and saw a Ford truck with a stake body roar off in the direction of St. Johnsbury.

So much for paperwork. I dropped my pen, jumped up, raced up the hallway, grabbed my gear and ran to my truck. I cranked the key and headed over to the farm, less than 10 minutes away, to investigate.

It didn't take me long to spot fresh tire tracks in the soft earth at the edge of the dirt road. I pulled over, got out, turned on my flashlight and shined it into the field. I spotted a dead doe, lying maybe 50 yards from the road, just 12 feet from the safety of the woods.

I walked over and placed my hand on the carcass. The doe was still warm. She had been killed very recently.

These guys were likely miles away, their truck parked out back of a home or inside a garage. But experience told me they would come back sometime tonight to pick up the deer.

I had to get out of the field and get my truck off the road fast. If they had any indication a warden had visited the field and found the doe, they would probably abandon the animal.

I needed to act fast to set a trap for the poachers. I knew I might be able to nab them alone, but to make certain they could not get away, I wanted more guys here.

Trouble was, Deputies Walt Ackermann and Dave Stevenson were over in Peacham, staking out an area where we had reports of poaching. They were a half hour's drive away from me.

How we got messages to one another before the advent of wireless communications seems extremely primitive compared to technology today. But it was all we had.

Basically, I had to call into the Dispatcher and ask her to relay my message. My deputies had a two way radio in their truck. But anything the Dispatcher said could be heard by people with a police scanner.

The public loved scanners, because they would know where the Fire Department was headed when the alarm sounded. But poachers used scanners to help them plot their night hunts.

For instance, if a poacher heard the Dispatcher report that wardens were working a certain area in Danville, they would drive several towns away to hunt back roads and shine a light. They used the public airwaves against us.

So, we came up with code words and code locations. The trick was to remember them all, to be able to tell the difference between a coded message and one that wasn't.

For instance, I might ask the Dispatcher to relay, "Warden Denton wants you to meet him at the Marshfield Dam." Walt and Dave and I would have agreed that Marshfield Dam was code for an entirely different spot, several towns away. Poachers would be thrown off and we would better our chances of catching them.

This night, I called the Dispatcher and used code for where I would meet up with Dave and Walt, figuring they would know what I meant. They didn't.

I waited, sitting up on a knoll above the dead doe, cold seeping into my bones, hoping whoever had shot her would wait to return until I had my deputies here to help me.

The goal was always to block all means of escape. If there were more than one person involved, a passenger would often leap out of a vehicle and make a run for it. A warden could generally nab the driver, but sometimes passengers bolted off into the pucker brush. A warden working alone would likely lose the second fellow.

This night, we had a couple of challenges. First off, Walt was driving his truck and it had

a noisy muffler. And Dave had a cast on his
leg. He would be worthless in a foot chase.
But you work with what you have.

After nearly an hour on the knoll, with frost
settling in and my behind going numb, I knew
something wasn't right. Dave and Walt should
have arrived by now.

Did they forget the code? Did I need to sneak
down to my truck and make another call
through the Dispatcher? What if the poachers
were listening in? How could I tell the guys
where I really was, without telling them?
I didn't want the fellows who had shot the doe
to know where I was. It would kill our chance
of catching them if they used a scanner.

Another five minutes went by.

I reluctantly got up out of my hiding spot and
started snaking my way down through the
brush towards my truck. I would relay another
coded message.

I began to wonder if this was a one man code.

It took another hour before Walt and Dave and
I were finally together and we had our game

plan. They were seated in their truck, which was backed into the woods to the north of the doe, hidden from the road.

I ran down the edge of the woods, planning to get south of the deer. I ducked into the trees at the edge of the field, headed for my spy spot on the hillside, when I heard the sound of tires and saw the trees around me light up from headlights.

I was so close to the open field, so close to the carcass! If a bright light shined the area, they would surely see me. I spotted a tiny grove of twisty cedars, stepped into them and pinned my back to the bark of the widest tree.

I was no more than 10 feet away from the doe.

The vehicle came down the road at a crawl. I could not make out what it was, but the lights were a foot or two lower than a truck's. It had to be a car. It stopped at the entrance to the field. The dome light came on inside the car when the front passenger door opened.

It was some sort of small hatchback. I had never seen deerjackers use one. They'd never be able to outrun a warden's car. And because the hatch had glass over the storage area, behind the backseat, anyone looking inside would see a dead deer—if you could even jam a carcass in there.

No way could this be the vehicle carrying our poachers.  Maybe it was kids out for a late night joy ride or some young couple looking for some privacy.

"I guess someone in that car has to pee," I murmured to myself.  "But of all the places to stop!"

To have this car squatting in the middle of our stakeout was like spending hours waxing your car only to have a flock of seagulls target it at the beach an hour later.

I poked my nose around a tree bough and watched as the back door opened and two people stepped into the roadway.  Both were wearing dark clothing, dressed for the weather.

One of them turned back to the car, bent down behind the rear passenger door and grabbed something.  The two figures looked up and down the road, talking to one

another, but too far away for me to hear
a word.

I didn't understand why they needed to talk
about taking a leak. "Come on. Pee! Get outta
here. Now!" I muttered beneath my breath.

But they didn't pee and they didn't leave.
Instead, one fellow turned on a narrow
flashlight beam, stepped over the ditch and
headed into the meadow. He swung the beam
back and forth in front of his feet to see his
way and headed right at me, with the other
man following behind.

I couldn't believe it. I wondered how they
planned to put that big doe into that little car.

Tie it to the hood? To the roof?

The car tires began to move. The driver was
slowly headed down the road towards me,
leaving the men behind. I peered into the
dark, trying to make out the car and license
plate number between the tree boughs. It was
a hatchback all right and from Vermont.

This was no time to jump out of the trees and
tell these two guys they were under arrest.

I wanted to catch everyone in the car. They might attempt to run away. I had to stay put, stand as still as I could, watch and wait.

Their voices got louder as the flashlight beam got closer. Definitely two males. One had a light beard. The other fellow moved easier and appeared 20 years younger. They were speaking Quebecois.

They talked so fast I had no idea what they were saying. I kicked myself for not taking French in high school. That night, I really could have used it.

When they found the doe, the older fellow reached beneath his coat and pulled out a skinning knife. The younger man unfolded two heavy duty black garbage bags and laid them on the grass.

Now, their plan was clear to me. They would cut up the deer, put the meat in the bags and carry them out. That's how a big doe fits in a tiny car. It was a bold plan because cutting up a deer takes time.

They obviously thought no game warden would find them.

I stood frozen, my hands at my sides like one of the Queen's Guard outside Buckingham Palace.

The fellows each grabbed a hoof and turned the deer onto her back and set to work. There was no fumbling about, no disagreement. They were like meat cutters who had worked side by side in a butcher shop for years. All that was missing was a big roll of white paper and their aprons.

They chatted and chuckled as slabs of meat slid neatly into the garbage bags. They could have been picking potatoes. After a half hour or so, the fellow with the knife let out a big sigh, straightened his back and the younger fellow turned off the small light.

For the first time since they stood over the carcass, they were silent. I was afraid they might hear me breathing behind them. I prayed my stomach didn't rumble. The older man reached inside his coat and pulled out a pack of cigarettes and offered one to his companion.

They both lit up and their conversation became even more animated. The older fellow

used his hands to punctuate his sentences—
the bloody blade whirled around in the dark.

When they were done with their cigarettes,
they went back to work.  They stuffed the bags
with meat, set them aside in the grass, then
dragged what was left of the doe into the trees,
just 15 feet from where I was standing.

They walked back to the bags, heavy with
fresh venison, stood and turned to look at the
road.  They continued to swap stories while
waiting for their getaway car to return.

With their backs facing me, I could breathe a
little easier, but I still could not move for fear
of breaking a twig with my boot or rustling the
branches all around me.  I didn't want to do
anything that might prompt them to look my
way and shine their light.

Their chatter stopped suddenly and their
heads shot up.  Headlights were coming.
The men ducked down into the grass and
stopped talking.

The vehicle slowed and came to a stop.  The
fellow with the flashlight jumped up, grabbed
the heaviest bag and tossed it over his

shoulder. He whispered to the older man, "C'est bon! Vite!" and passed him the smaller, lighter bag to carry. The two of them ran towards the car.

At last, it was time to pounce.

I waited until the poachers were half way through the meadow, then turned and slid through the woods and ran to the road. My goal was to get in front of the car, to stop it.

With the men at the vehicle, I pushed the button on my portable radio and told Walt and Dave, "Go! Go!" I expected them to come roaring down the hill with their headlights on and siren blaring, to scare the heck out of those guys.

But there was nothing. No action from the deputies. No noisy truck being fired up and rushing down the road. No radio response from them either.

I held the button again, harder and said louder, "Go! Go! Go!" Still nothing.

I had no idea what was going on with Dave and Walt, but I was determined to stop that car. I stepped into the road and saw the poacher's car picking up speed and headed right at me.

Forget the radio. I charged at the car like I was a bull seeing red. I yelled at the top of my lungs, "STOP! GAME WARDEN!!" hoping the driver would hit the brakes and Walt and Dave would finally hear me and come fast.

The car kept coming. I didn't know if the driver even saw me. I began running backwards and screaming at the driver to stop. I shouted to Walt and Dave.

At last, the driver hit the brakes. The car skidded a few feet, lurched forward, then settled.

I got right up into the grill, looked over the headlights and all I saw were eyeballs. They were huge and there were a lot of them. The people inside looked terrified. It looked to me like the meat cutters had brought their entire family with them.

Finally, Walt's noisy truck roared down the road. He turned his pickup sideways, so the driver could not turn around and attempt to escape.

Walt jumped out of the truck. It took Dave a bit longer, since his leg was in a cast.

"Didn't you guys hear me call you on the radio?" I asked Walt. "No. Nothing," he said. "We kept waiting. We came when we heard you yelling," he said.

Walt took one side of the hatchback and Dave took the other. They shined their lights inside, then opened the car doors.

The deputies found the vehicle packed with people, shoulder to shoulder. A woman was driving. There were three kids and a baby, along with the two fellows I saw cut up the deer.

We'd never seen night hunting turned into a family affair.

"There's two garbage bags of fresh venison in there somewhere," I told Walt. "Please, find them."

Walt and Dave looked around the car a few minutes. The passengers remained inside. There were so many people, we didn't want anyone running off. It was smarter to just keep them in the vehicle.

Walt came back to me again. "Nothing. We can't find anything," he told me. I looked over at Dave. He nodded in agreement with Walt.

I sighed. Nothing this night had gone smoothly.

"It has to be in there!" I hissed. "Look again!"

The deputies gave it another go. This time they got everyone out of the vehicle, a few at a time. They found the garbage bags, each tucked inside a grain bag, and placed on the backseat floorboards.

With the venison in our hands, I could prove a crime had been committed. I called the state police for assistance transporting the seven people to the St. Johnsbury barracks. I knew it would take time chatting with the adults to get to the bottom of this case.

At the barracks, we learned the men cutting up the deer were, indeed, from Quebec. The driver claimed one of the men said he needed a ride but didn't say why. She couldn't leave her kids alone, but wanted to help him. So, she loaded up all her children and just did what he told her.

I might not understand Quebecois, but I could tell when a fellow was in charge of a night hunt.

He fit.

I took the older fellow into a room for questioning. He was a tough nut to crack. He kept shaking his head, left to right, and saying, "No Anglais!" whenever we asked him anything.

I was determined not to let this guy walk because of the language barrier. I asked for an interpreter.

Under the bright lights of the interrogation room, the bearded man sat, alternately glaring at me and then staring at the tabletop. His arms were crossed, his lips sealed. It took two hours to get a qualified person to climb out of their warm bed and drive to the barracks to assist us.

When the interpreter stepped into the room, she smiled and introduced herself in Quebecois to him. His whole demeanor changed. He smiled at her and began talking, waving his arms and telling a long story. He stopped, pointed at me and glowered.

Following the outburst, she turned to me and summarized his statement. "He says he didn't do anything wrong."

It was close to 3 a.m. It had been a long night of ups and downs working to get the poachers. I had the venison. I had my own eye witness account.

But if he would not confess, if this went to a jury trial, what else might I need?

I stood and looked at him. The evidence was right there on his clothes. I took a deep breath and calmly asked the interpreter to explain to the suspect that I saw the dead doe's blood on his boots.

She repeated my words in Quebecois. He looked at her, then knitted his eyebrows together and slid his chair back a few inches to look down at his boots. He acted like he was surprised to learn there was blood on his boots.

He looked back up at me, his face feigning shock and innocence.

"Tell him I want his boots. For evidence. Tell him to take them off," I told her.

She repeated my words. He sat back in
his chair, stunned. He looked up at me
like he thought maybe I would reconsider.
I uncrossed my arms, pointed to his boots
and didn't so much as blink. "Now!" I
barked.

The woman jumped a little, turned to him
and said, "Immediatement!" in a softer tone.

Slowly, he bent over, untied the bootlaces,
slipped his feet out and put the boots
together.

Walt was sitting in a corner quietly, just
listening. He stood up, walked over and
picked up the boots, then went back to his
chair and set the evidence on the floor.

I looked hard at the fellow's coat. The cuffs
had blood on them. And there were dark
spatters on the front, near the pockets.

"Tell him his coat has bloodstains too. On
the cuffs and on the front. His coat is
evidence. I need it. Tell him to take off his
coat," I said to the interpreter.

Once again, she repeated my words.

The suspect turned to look up at me again.
He still looked angry, but not quite as defiant.

Walt silently took the jacket and put it with the boots.

"Tell him to put his hands flat on the table," I said. He listened to her repeat my words and did what he was asked. He kept his head down this time.

I took a couple steps forward and looked down at his long sleeve shirt beneath the bright light.

I saw bloodstains on the cuffs.

"There are bloodstains on his shirt," I said.

"Tell him his shirt is more evidence against him. Tell him to give us his shirt."

He listened to her explain my words.
His eyes widened. He was now without his coat, his boots and his shirt.

It was below zero outside with a light snow falling, around 4 a.m. Still, this guy refused to confess to what I had seen him do.

I needed evidence, a lot of it, to prove his guilt to a judge or jury.

I turned to the interpreter again. "Tell him to stand up, please."

The woman translated and the fellow slowly pushed back his chair. He climbed to his feet like a guy with a bad back. Both palms remained flat on the tabletop.

His head was down. It was late. We were all tired.

I walked over and stood two feet from him. I saw more blood spattered on the front of his trousers, even a few wisps of deer hair sticking to the dried blood.

"Tell him I see blood and deer hair on his trousers. Evidence," I told the interpreter. "Tell him to take off his pants."

The interpreter turned to the fellow, took a deep breath and was just about to open her mouth to translate when the bearded man stood straight up, turned and looked at me.

His eyes were as big as saucers.

He rocked back on his heels, stared at me, and
in a voice both indignant and astonished said,
"The pants too?"

So much for the language barrier.

He walked out of the barracks a little before
5 a.m., wearing just his socks and longjohns.
His elbows pumped the cold night air.

I stood at the window and saw him grip the
citation so tight, it was like he was trying to
strangle it.

He slid into the passenger seat of a waiting
car, turned his head and shouted something
in Quebecois at the barracks and slammed his
door shut.

"Hunh," I said to myself, "I guess it's a good
thing I never learned French."

*I certainly did want to
get inside their camp.
I wanted to find evidence
someone had stashed
an illegal deer.*

# BAG YER BUCK

CONTRIBUTED BY TERRY WILLIAMS

Back in the 1940s, over in East Poultney, a farmer gave a persistent fellow permission to erect a hunting camp in the middle of his 100 plus acres.

Decades passed. The farmer died. The hunter's family grew. The camp saw a lot more use. It evolved into a year round home away from home for the original hunter and a half dozen of his adult children, their kids and their many friends. There was noisy squabbling among the campers, and a lot of traffic going in and out of the cabin at all hours of the day and night.

The elderly widow, along with a family friend who served as a caretaker, decided they'd had enough. They wanted the tenancy ended. But the agreement made by her late husband said the camp could remain there as long as it stood. She couldn't just throw them off her land.

After chatting with an attorney about what she could do, the caretaker posted her acreage against hunting and trespass. Now, the family had their camp, but to legally hunt they had to drive down the road and find land that was not posted.

Someone didn't like being kept off her land. They were ignoring the No Trespass signs. The widow and caretaker didn't know who was coming onto the property, but they wanted it to stop. The game warden's phone began ringing with complaints. The owner was asking for help.

It was deer season—always the busiest time of year for wardens. My supervisor, Warden Norm Brown of Wells, asked me to check into the situation.

"Just take a walk and get a feel for what's going on and let me know what you find out," Norm said.

The next morning, I headed out for a visit. It was the middle of the first week of deer season. The serious deer hunters—the fellows who take time off from their day jobs to hunt—were out there.

My plan was to step into the woods around 10 a.m. That way I'd see the tracks of all the fellows who had been out in the woods hunting since dawn.

I wasn't wearing my uniform. I dressed to blend in with the other hunters. Some blaze orange, my rifle over my shoulder and warm clothing.

There were lots of local people who knew me, of course. And many of them knew I worked as a part time deputy warden in addition to my full time job in nearby Rutland City. But whether I was hunting deer or hunting the hunters—no one but Norm and I knew.

I parked a quarter of a mile away from the property I intended to visit and backed up so it would be difficult for a passing driver to spot my car. Parking a good distance away made it hard for anyone to figure out why I was in the area.

My badge was pinned to my shirt, but hidden beneath my coat. When I climbed out of my car, I slung my deer rifle over my shoulder.

Off I went for a little walk.

It had been a wet Autumn. Tire tracks and boot prints would be easy to spot.

Even better, a few inches of snow had fallen overnight, covering the ground like flour. If anyone had been trespassing on this posted land, it would be easy to find the tracks today and follow them back to their source.

But my first job was to make certain the land was legally posted.

I walked up over a hill, down into a pretty valley and immediately saw new "No Trespassing" signs posted along the border, signed and properly spaced.

I had checked the town clerk's office earlier. Vermont law required a bit of paperwork there too.

Looking at the signage, it was clear the caretaker had followed the law.

Now the question was, were people respecting the landowner's wishes?

I walked inside the posted property and followed the boundary lines, searching for boot prints and any other signs of trespass.

There were several hunting camps in the area. While I knew the big family with the camp would not be happy having the land around them put off limits, just exactly who was trespassing remained to be seen.

I walked about half the property line when I
spied the tracks of a small deer and 50 yards
further on, a few drops of blood in the snow.

Someone had shot a deer inside the landowner's
posted property this morning.

I followed the tracks and within another 70 yards
I found where the deer had fallen.  I could tell by
the small hoof prints and the impression its body
left in the snow it was little more than a fawn.
"Skippers" we call the little ones.

The odds of a deer this size having antlers long
enough to make it a legal kill, for a hunter to tag
and report it as required by law, were about nil.

I kept walking, following the story in the snow.

Someone had backed a truck up to within 40
feet of the carcass.  It was clear from the prints
one man had stepped out of the truck, walked
over and loaded the little deer into the vehicle
and driven away.

Most hunters are embarrassed to admit they
shot a deer that size.  But wardens know there
are fellows who will shoot any deer, to turn them
into camp meat.  Some fellows figure it saves
on buying protein for the crew while they are in

camp looking for bigger animals for the freezer or a trophy to hang on their wall.

Guys that do this play with fire.  They are hoping a warden won't catch them.

That's what I figured had happened here.

I followed the tire tracks over the hill, through a sugar maple stand, and around a bend.  The tracks turned onto a more heavily traveled lane, churned deep by big truck tires.

I walked the edge of the ruts and came upon a simple hunting camp with board and batten siding.  It was about 24 feet square, gray with age and sitting not quite level atop a combination of cement blocks and stones.  Four trucks were parked in some weeds 30 or more feet away.

I recognized two of the trucks as belonging to guys whose names I knew.  They were part of a rowdy family, who liked to yelp and roar and occasionally, brawl.

I'd landed at the Badger Boys camp.  This was the family that had the camp lease, the widow's prime suspect for trespassing and hunting on her land.

I knew the men a little. They were serious about hunting, always thinking they had to do better than everybody else. They reacted to deer rifle season like some little kids go nuts for Christmas, counting down from Halloween— maybe even Easter.

Clothes, guns, ammo, vehicles, down to the stickers on their truck bumpers and for all I knew, their underwear, made clear they lived for deer hunting.

Oh, they went after turkeys and geese and ducks too. But it was mostly just to stay in practice. Deer and talking about them, dreaming about them, bragging about who got the biggest one—and mercilessly teasing any fellow who missed a shot at a good buck—was the center of their lives.

They were so competitive with their disparate opinions as to the best rifle, the best ammo, still hunt or stalk—it was just about impossible for them to tolerate other points of view. Some brother was always angry with another one or two.

Wisely, the Badgers were smart enough to keep their battles inside the family. They didn't want to risk ending up in jail. That could mean they might miss all or part of a hunting season.

I took a deep breath realizing this visit was going to require some finesse.

As I picked my way over the ruts, headed to the cabin door, I saw a window shade move a couple inches to the left.  Someone had spotted me.

In another three steps, George Badger stepped out of the camp and called to me.

"Stop right there!" he said.  "What do you want?"

I was 15 feet from the entrance.  I knew George from my football days in high school.  He had been on an opposing team.  He wasn't big, but he was scrappy.

I smiled, slowed my walk but kept coming.
I said cheerily, "Hi, George! You remember me. It's Terry Williams.  I'm just out checking..." and now I was standing at the bottom of the porch steps.

"You stay right there," he said, interrupting me. "We can talk from here."

We chatted about the weather and the hunting. George softened a bit.  But he didn't invite me to come any closer.  It was clear to me he didn't want me inside the camp.

I adjusted my rifle on my shoulder and leaned on the handrail as we talked. Now and again, I glanced down for blood on the steps. I was certain that little deer was inside this camp. But I didn't have a search warrant. I couldn't enter the cabin unless invited.

And while I intended to chat with George and whoever else was inside about respecting their neighbor's land rights, I wanted to be polite and ease into the subject.

I looked over at the pickup trucks. They were all parked too far away—covered in mud and their tailgates up—to spy a tiny drop of blood on a bumper.

George and I chatted maybe 10 minutes, when the camp door opened wide. The white haired patron of the Badger clan strolled out onto the deck in thick wool socks, suspenders over his green Johnson wool trousers and a big smile plastered on his face.

"Well! What do you know," he said like he had a bit part in a school play.

He pretended it was a big surprise to find me outside speaking with his son. "I thought I heard Georgie talking to somebody out here," Willis Badger said.

The camp patriarch turned to George, scowled theatrically and said, "What're you doing out here in the cold? What's wrong with you? Why didn't you invite Terry inside to warm up?" And he raised his arm like he was going to swat his son.

George was used to it. He had probably been smacked since he was old enough to walk. The old man let fly a slow backhand. George tucked his chin to his chest and leaned back six inches, let it go by and scowled. The old man winked at me and chuckled.

"Come on in, Terry," the elder said with a big smile. "Come on in and say hello to the boys and warm up."

Well, I certainly did want to get inside their camp. I wanted to find evidence someone had stashed an illegal deer. I nodded, said, "Thank you," and stepped up onto the porch.

The elder Badger opened the door wide for me. I was immediately hit with the smell of wet leather boots, sweat, gun oil, coffee and wood smoke.

The camp was just two rooms with a loft above for more sleeping and some storage. Before me, was a worn table laden with loaves of bread, boxes of crackers, a big wheel of cheese, knives, forks, butter and napkins.

In the living area were a couple of tattered couches with throws over them to hide the stuffing poking out of sagging cushions. A couple of guys were playing cards at a small table. Another fellow was sprawled out on the couch with a blanket over him sleeping, while another smaller guy was in a dark corner, buried deep in a sleeping bag.

I took off my hat and stamped the snow off my boots.

"Sorry about the mud and snow on my boots," I said, looking down at the floor—not for snow, but for a drop or two of blood and maybe some wisps of deer hair from the skipper.

"Eh, don't worry about it," the old man said. "Come on in and have something to eat."

"It'll just take a minute to kick them off," I said. "I don't want to get water all over your floor." I bent down and started unlacing my boots. It was my chance to look for evidence.

The noise of me entering camp prompted the fellow on the couch to grab a corner of his blanket, roll over and turn his back to us. But whoever was in the sleeping bag didn't stir.

"I guess we should try and be a little more quiet, eh?" the old man said in a near whisper to George and me with a little smile on his face.

"A couple of the boys were up and out before dawn, trying to get set up on some big tracks they found earlier down the road. They're planning on driving back there later today."

He knew he was telling me something I wanted to hear—they hadn't been on the newly posted land surrounding their camp. They were driving to other locations. He was smart.

"Had any luck so far?" I asked him.

"No," he said, shaking his head. "No luck yet. But we've got plenty of time. And in a few hours, the boys will be out there again."

He changed the subject to food. "Now, what can I get you?" he said. He ran through a list of beverages from root beer to rum and invited me to sit at the kitchen table.

"No alcohol for me, thanks. I'm on duty," I told him. I didn't think they would forget a deputy warden was visiting, but I thought I'd say it plainly.

"I'll take some black coffee and a slice of that cheese, maybe a couple of crackers," I said to be polite, and pulled up a chair. Every deer camp had a coffee pot going and I smelled it when I stepped in. I also saw they had plenty of cheese and enough crackers to supply a church supper. So, I wasn't asking them to do any work and it would be impolite to refuse.

One of the Badgers pulled a long, curved hunting knife from his belt, and before I could stop him, he sliced a hunk of cheese big enough to keep a mouse happy for five years.

"Whoa! You take most of that," I said. "That's very kind, but I don't need that much!" He grinned, nodded and artfully sliced the piece in thirds. He speared a piece, lifted it into the air with the tip of his knife and held it there. I reached over and picked it off the blade and said, "Thank you."

"We have a friend who works at Cabot Cheese up north," the young man piped up. "He gets us a good price on a wheel every year."

I took a bite and listened as the wood stove sizzled and popped. "It's great cheese, all right," I said.

I sipped my coffee, picked up a couple of crackers and made a sandwich by placing some of the cheese in the middle.

I chatted a good 10 minutes with the Badger boys about everything from the best bread for a toasted cheese sandwich to local sports. The fellow snuggled into the back of the sofa began to snore.

I glanced a time or two at the guy in the sleeping bag in the dark corner, to see if there was any movement there. He didn't stir.

I took a deep breath and brought up the topic of respecting posted property and staying off land with No Trespassing signs.

There was some angry sputtering from the Badgers. The cracker boxes rocked like skyscrapers in an earthquake when the old man slammed a closed fist down on the tabletop, saying he'd been walking and hunting the land around him for 40 years.

I didn't argue with anyone. I just reminded them it was the landowner's right to post their land. They owned it. Paid the taxes. Everyone had to respect the law.

I stood up, thanked them for their hospitality, laced up my boots, picked up my rifle and walked out the door, headed for home.

I wanted to get ahold of Norm, to tell him about the little deer I knew was hidden in that camp, to convince him to get a search warrant.

Thing was, deputy wardens years ago didn't have radios or any way to get ahold of a boss. I was pretty certain Norm would be out in the woods checking the licenses of deer hunters or following up on another complaint. I'd have to hike back to my car, get to a landline phone and start calling around to even begin to locate him.

When I finally caught up with Norm, it was early afternoon. I explained to the boss what I had seen and said, "Let's get a warrant and go back there."

Norm looked at his watch, sighed and shook his head.

"Terry, those guys would have gotten rid of the evidence by now—cleaned it all up. They're smart. They probably ran the truck through a car wash and stashed the venison in a friend's house miles away. The head, the hide, the hooves, it's all long gone. I'm sorry, Terry, but we'll never get them on this one."

I knew Norm was probably right, but it still hurt. There was no doubt in my mind someone in that camp had trespassed onto the widow's land that morning, shot a fawn, tossed it into the back of a truck and driven it to the Badger's camp.

We could have gotten them for taking an illegal deer, maybe even proved they shot it on their neighbor's posted land, if only we could have acted faster.

I just had to let it go.

Rifle season ended. Christmas came and went. It was January and I was slogging my way down Poultney's Main Street, headed to the auto parts store. I heard someone behind me yell, "Terry!" and turned to see a fellow trotting towards me.

Roger Badger swaggered up to me with a big grin on his face and a glint in his eyes. His head was covered in a fur lined cap, pulled right down over his ears.

"Hi, Roger. How are you?" I said, clapping my mittened hands together and smiling.

"Anybody ever tell you you're an idiot?" he said, getting right up under my chin. He was a head shorter than me and that was the best he could do to try and intimidate me.

"I've been called worse," I said and shrugged.

I wasn't about to let him bother me. Still, I wondered why he had to pick one of the coldest days of the year to stop and insult me. Couldn't he wait for a nice summer day? What did he really want?

"Well, you are an idiot. You have to be an idiot," he said. "You came right inside our camp and you still didn't figure it out." He grinned and took a step back, awaiting my reaction.

"Are you talking about the skipper you guys killed and hid in the sleeping bag?" I said calmly.

"You knew?" he gasped with surprise. His mouth opened wide showing a tangle of teeth only a dentist should have to witness.

"Of course, I knew," I said.

"Well, then why didn't you do something about it? How come you didn't come back with a search warrant?" he shouted.

I looked at him and let a little smile come across my face, like I had a secret. I didn't say a word. I wanted him to talk. It was clear he was dying to say something.

"After you left camp, everyone started arguing about what we should do," Roger said. We figured you'd be back with a warrant in an hour or two and bring Norm or maybe even the state police. Al and Jim just up and grabbed their rifles, jumped into their trucks and took off. They didn't come back the rest of deer season. They say they're done," Roger said, shaking his head.

He gave me a look like I was the skunk that showed up for dinner.

He took a deep breath, looked down at the snow and continued.

"Those of us who stayed behind, we got rid of—well, you know—and then we took turns looking out the window. Night and day! Nobody slept. Everybody was fighting," his voice trailed off, thinking about all the turmoil.

Then he looked up into my face again, his cheeks red from the wind, and said, "And you never even came back!" He spit on the snow, a couple inches from my boot, leaned in and jutted his chin back up under mine.

He reminded me of a feisty little terrier.

I imagined the Badgers bickering, the camp door slamming. It gave me some satisfaction. But not as much as citing whoever killed that little deer.

I said, "We're always watching, Roger," smiled, stepped around him and went on my way.

Winter was long. Then in late April, after two days of warm Spring rains, there was a fire call in town.

Something was ablaze in the East Poultney woods.

It was the Badger Boys camp. And all the ruts and low branches and churned up mud from the trucks going in and out made it impossible for the fire trucks to get up the trail.

The camp burned to the ground.  But why?

The story I heard was the wife of one of the
Badgers learned her husband was having an
affair with a woman half her age.  He was
using the hunting camp for his romantic
rendezvous.

Mrs. Badger had learned a thing or two about
tracking after hearing the men's endless deer
stalking tales.  She went looking for his truck.

She found out what he was up to.

And the next time he called home to say,
"Geez, Honey.  I'm sorry but I have to work late
again," she was ready.

She hiked into the camp with a can of gas in
one hand and a cigarette lighter in the other,
saw his truck outside and set the place on fire.

The lovebirds ran buck naked out of the cabin,
off into the woods.

The old hunting camp went up like a torch.
Burned down to the cinderblocks.  Nothing left
but ashes.

With their camp gone, the Badgers' agreement
with the beleaguered landowner was finally
over.

The Badger Boys moved on.

The widow got what she wanted—the peaceable
enjoyment of her land.

Her calls to Norm, to stop the trespassing,
ended.

When I heard about the fire, I pondered how
this had worked out.

It struck me, maybe justice isn't only dealt
by law officers handing out citations, making
fellows stand before a judge, pay a fine or even
spend some time in jail.

You wait long enough, Life happens.  Somebody
else takes care of things.

# Acknowledgements

*This book could not have been completed without the encouragement and skill of the following individuals:*

**Jean McHenry**
**Sam Stanley**
**Dorrice and John Hammer**
**Inge Schaefer**
**Sandra Brisson**
**Al and Karen Meyers**
**Jean Cross**
**Bethany Greeley Knight**
**Debra Russell Sanborn**
**and O.C.**

*Thank you, one and all.*

# Many thanks to the following for...

 **John Kapusta** worked 38 years as a Vermont warden. John resides in Hardwick.

 **Eric Nuse** worked 32 years as a Vermont warden. Eric resides in Johnson.

 **Bob Lutz** worked 23 years as a Vermont warden. Bob resides in Fairfax.

 **Ken Denton** worked 30 years as a Vermont warden. Ken resides in Cabot.

# ...ALLOWING ME TO SHARE THEIR STORIES

 **Walt Ackermann** worked 19 years as a deputy warden. Walt resides in Cabot.

 **Norm Brown** worked 35 years as a Vermont warden. Norm resides in Wells.

 **Terry Williams** worked 10 years as a deputy warden. Terry resides in Poultney.

# Stories By Warden

**John Kapusta**
CADILLAC JACK
BRUISIN' & CHEWIN'

**Eric Nuse**
BUTTON UP

**Bob Lutz**
YOU BROKE IT...

**Ken Denton**
SHANTY SURPRISE
SNOW GLOBE
LOVE MY GUN
MAD MOOSE
COLD COMFORT
NO ANGLAIS

**Walt Ackermann**
SHANTY SURPRISE
COLD COMFORT
NO ANGLAIS

**Norm Brown**
DOUG'S DEN
DOUG'S DONE

**Terry Williams**
BAG YER BUCK